W9-DEV-542

African-American Stories
of Triumph Over Adversity

African-American Stories of Triumph Over Adversity

Joy Cometh in the Morning

GERALDINE COLEMAN

Foreword by Phyllis Cunningham

BERGIN & GARVEY
Westport, Connecticut • London

Library of Congress Cataloging-in-Publication Data

Coleman, Geraldine.
    African-American stories of triumph over adversity : joy cometh
  in the morning / Geraldine Coleman ; foreword by Phyllis Cunningham.
        p.   cm.
    Includes bibliographical references (p.   ) and index.
    ISBN 0–89789–505–3 (alk. paper)
    1. Afro-Americans—Biography.   2. Success—United States.
  I. Title.
  E185.96.C63   1996
  973′.0496073′022—dc20   96–906

British Library Cataloguing in Publication Data is available.

Library of Congress Catalog Card Number: 96–906
ISBN: 0–89789–505–3

First published in 1996

Bergin & Garvey, 88 Post Road West, Westport, CT 06881
An imprint of Greenwood Publishing Group, Inc.

Printed in the United States of America

The paper used in this book complies with the
Permanent Paper Standard issued by the National
Information Standards Organization (Z39.48–1984).

10 9 8 7 6 5 4 3 2 1

For my parents,
Charles and Ernestine Coleman,
who by their example taught me
no mountain is too high to climb,
no river too wide to cross

weeping may endure for a night,
but joy cometh in the morning

Psalms 30:5

Contents

viii   Contents

Foreword

African-American scholars who reflect on concerns or concepts that are educational issues for their community often marvel at the fortitude, the resilience, the focus on possibility that characterize ordinary black folks. We are not talking about the heroes, the leaders, those gifted in extraordinary ways but those ordinary members of the community who make up the race and who are the everyday heroes that signify what it means to be black and proud.

Interest in and pride about African-Americans who have made it despite the barriers, the inordinate surfacing of race in the crooks and crannies of life in the United States, and the struggle for survival was clearly a topic to explore for Geraldine Coleman. She had her share of these same struggles, but she did not see herself as a victim. Characterized by a healthy and clear understanding of who she is and the nature of the society in which she lives, Geri wanted to explore those lives that she knew about in a surface way by giving voice to those who lived them. It is from their voices, the sixteen persons whom we hear telling their life stories, voices which, though personal are also political, that we learn how family, and society and its structure take on meaning in their experiencing of life.

We also are challenged to redefine success. Each of the persons interviewed felt successful in life and all had taken charge of their lives and had their own definition of what it meant to enjoy success.

Joy Cometh in the Morning is a start for African- and Euro-Americans to celebrate blackness and the contribution to our history, our values, our cultures by ordinary African-Americans. Each of us needs to evaluate what it means to be different in our society and what it means to find unity in diversity by seeking out the ordinary and letting those voices be heard.

Preface

In the initial stages of the evolution of this book, the most difficult task was the selection of a research topic. My choices were governed by a desire to engage in research that would be of value to both the academic and lay communities. I wanted to add to the body of knowledge on triumph over adversity that could guide the practice of diverse institutions, as well as serve as a source of inspiration for individuals in the throes of personal struggles.

In recent years a number of books of this genre have been published. However, this book's uniqueness is grounded in the diversity of its subjects and the issues addressed. Its subjects are male and female; they represent ages that span several decades and come from many different walks of life. Rather than focusing on a particular time period in their lives, the focus is on the extended time line that allows the reader to experience the psychological evolution of each storyteller.

There were a number of ways in which I could have given voice to the storytellers. However, I chose oral histories because, by their very nature, they contextualize issues and enhance their meaning. Oral history breathes life into the written word, adding depth and richness. Similarly, metaphors are used extensively in the final chapters. Metaphors add color to our thoughts, giving them dimension. They form images of our emotions giving them texture and substance.

The oral tradition was a significant part of African cultures. The village griot (storyteller) was held in high esteem. This tradition took root among many African-Americans as well, and therefore seemed a befitting way to have them share their experiences with the reader. I, too, acquired a knowledge of my ancestors at the knee of my mother and father who, for as long as I can remember, connected their children with their past in this manner. There was the story of my great-great-grandfather who was a habitual runaway and was sold down river because he refused to surrender, mind, body, and spirit, to the dehumanizing machinations of slavery, and of my father who, as a boy of barely fourteen years old, fled the oppressive social conditions of the South and traveled north in pursuit of opportunities to realize his potential and fulfill his hopes and dreams. They were the family griots who told these and many other stories to their children, grandchildren and great-grandchildren, connecting the later generations to the past, and helping them to define themselves. It was the impact of this personal experience that contributed to my decision to use oral history to give voice to the storytellers.

Oral history is "verbal stories passed on from one generation to the next" (Hoopes, 1979, p. 6). While oral history is as old as history itself, its use as a research methodology is relatively new (Thompson, 1988). Since the oral tradition predated recorded history, oral history was in fact the first kind of history.

The oral tradition in Africa is complex. It is divided into five categories: (1) learning titles, rituals and formulas, (2) learning lists of places and personal names, (3) learning official and private poetry, (4) learning stories, and (5) learning legal commentaries (Vansina, 1961). So important was the oral tradition in these cultures that a formalized system was developed to ensure content consistency as the stories were passed from generation to generation. These too took various forms ranging from schools designed specifically to teach traditional lore, a competency test of sorts, which required the individual to recite from any of the previously mentioned categories prior to taking office, disputations, and the like. It was found that the stories were retained with amazing accuracy for generations. The oral tradition was not limited to African cultures. Its counterpart is found in the Scandinavian skald and the indian Rajput (Vansina, 1961, p. 24).

The most famous testimonial to the oral tradition is, of course, Alex Haley's *Roots* (1976). Haley's quest to discover his ancestral roots began with a griot. Haley recalled his first impression upon seeing the griot. His dress and countenance projected an air of importance. After telling Haley the story of his ancestor, Kunta Kinte, Haley revealed notes from a story told to him by his grandmother—the same story. This oral tradition remains in many black families today.

Unlike the oral tradition previously discussed that consists of a story passed down from generation to generation, the oral histories presented here consist of the spoken memories of all aspects of the storyteller's life. This type of oral history is more characteristic of literate societies (Hoopes, 1992). Oral history, unlike data gathered using traditional methodologies such as books, letters, diaries, deeds, census records, and other artifacts, personalizes history. It gives voice to the past. Hoopes notes that oral history is also based on documents. However, these "documents" are verbal and consist of the verbal word, folklore, songs, speeches, interviews, and formal and informal conversations (Hoopes, 1979). Oral history allows the writer to truly capture the spirit of the people.

Acknowledgments

Few achieve success without having walked in the shadow of knowing and caring others. It has been my good fortune to have walked in the shadow of many competent and caring individuals. I have benefited from their knowledge and learned the nuances of scholarly research from their example. I acquired a thirst for knowledge and the discipline to seek its hiding places. For this, I am most indebted to Phyllis Cunningham, Mike Salovesh, and Jorge Jeria. Each contributed something special to this research to bring it to fruition. Thank you, Dr. Cunningham, for your constant encouragement and your sharp intellect and the ability to quickly and succinctly grasp the root of a problem and set me on the right course; Dr. Salovesh, for teaching me the technicalities of data collection and the meaning of the word "patience," and Dr. Jeria, for inspiring a sensitivity to listening to the silence to capture the spirit.

My journey has been long but rewarding. Therefore, I would be remiss in not mentioning my parents and all of those inspiring African-American elementary, junior high, and high school teachers, who refused to allow me to question my abilities and consistently pushed and encouraged me to set and reach very ambitious goals in life. A special thank you to my mentors, James Y. Peoples and Patricia Welch, for your uncompromising support and encouragement in my professional life.

I am indebted to my family and friends for their support and genuine expressions of interest in this research. Special thanks to Bill Davies, Kevin Seidel, Pat Krakar, and Gwen Johnson who devoted personal time to assisting me in converting computer disks and set-up; Janice Cleaves, who did a superb job of transcribing tapes; Vanessa Harris for preparing this manuscript for copy; Ava Evbuoma for editing a particularly challenging transcript and being my resident expert on all the little things that matter; Eulaletta Johnson-Pickett; Andrea Foster and Lorna Anderson, who sought out individuals with fascinating stories to tell and directed them to me, and the storytellers themselves for allowing me to enter the private recesses of their lives.

There are some people in our lives we can count on to come to our aid, no matter the season. They are there in good times and in bad. I owe an extra special thanks to my sister and brother-in-law, Bernice and James Lloyd, for being my savior in the eleventh hour, xeroxing, proofreading, in general, assisting in tying up the loose ends.

Part I

METAMORPHOSIS

1

Introduction

This book is about ordinary people and the structures in their families, schools, and communities that have assisted them in getting beyond adversity to live successful and productive lives. It is a journey from darkness into the light. Our storytellers emerge with a "knowing" that weeping may endure for a night but joy cometh in the morning. It is grounded in an Afrocentric perspective, as they speak from the perspective of living in black skin in a society where skin color is imbued with social meaning.

It is an ethnographic study in which themes were extracted from the oral histories of sixteen African-Americans, using ideas utilized by the phenomenologist Herbert Spiegelberg. We embark on a journey through the pages of the life of each storyteller. Along the way, we examine the relationship between the interpretation of social reality and the ability to conquer adversity. We seek answers to the question of why some individuals are able to overcome adversity and others, who labor under the same or similar circumstances, are not.

Four primary themes emerged. They were family roots, support systems, resistance, and spirituality. The stories provide strong support for concluding that success in conquering adversity could be attributed to such variables as families with clearly articulated values, support from significant others, strong will, positive self-concept, and religious faith.

Family, school, and community formed the conceptual framework from which the stories unfold. These were selected, as they reflect the primary institutional settings in which social interaction occurs.

In addition to grappling with the many problems that accompany each life stage, the African-American carries the additional burden of race. For the African-American, skin color is an indelible mark of inferior social status.

Consequently, the struggles that we can each expect to encounter as we travel along life's pathway are oftentimes exacerbated by issues of race. The pathway to success is often strewn with obstacles and maneuvering around these obstacles makes the journey more burdensome. Consequently, some do not successfully complete the journey; others are so discouraged by what lies ahead, that they do not attempt to make the journey. Then there are those who recognize the challenge before them, survey the course, maneuver around the obstacles, and reach their destination.

It is the latter that have been heralded by the dominant culture as role models. It is this group that the dominant culture uses to attenuate charges of racial discrimination—"You see, they did it. Why can't you?" Consequently, the tendency has been to blame the victim and not a social structure that creates an underclass and systematically constructs and perpetuates a reality that makes it most difficult for them to achieve cultural goals through institutionalized means. This is the reality and the focus of this book. Given the extraneous problems associated with race, why do some individuals deal effectively with adversity in their lives and beat the odds, and others do not?

The selection of the subject matter of this book was, in part, driven by my own personal experiences. There are those who hold that what we choose to write about is as much a reflection of our own biography as it is of the persons or issues we write about. Clearly, my personal experiences add to the validity of this belief. The choice of the subject matter is as much a tribute to the courage and determination of my parents, in their struggle and success in raising a large family with limited resources, as it is to the courageous individuals who allowed me to enter the most private recesses of their lives.

I have long admired the courage of such individuals who refuse to allow accident of birth, time, or circumstance to define their being and limit their possibilities. They possess an inner strength that keeps the flame of hope burning. They tend to live their lives by the philosophy that one is only limited by the possibilities and where there is a will, there is a way. Their perspective on life allows them to view obstacles in life as stepping-stones rather than stumbling blocks.

In the April 1992 issue of *Our Daily Bread* is a story that clearly illustrates this perspective on life. The story goes that there was a small boy mesmerized by the stirring of life in a cocoon. As he watched this marvel of nature unfold, he sympathized with the moth as it struggled to free itself from its prison. He responded as would any caring, sensitive person and slit the cocoon open to allow the moth to escape. However, to his dismay, the moth lacked its usual vibrancy and was unable to fly and before long it died. The boy did not understand the ways of nature, for the moth's struggle to free itself was essential to its development. It was through this tedious, seemingly painful process that essential body fluids are stimulated that give luster to its wings and enable it to fly.

The oral histories of the storytellers resonate with examples of the empowering effect of personal struggle. Each struggle was fortifying. With each struggle came the resolve to press forward. Their response to personal struggles was not to perceive them as barriers that block access to a goal and thus to give up. While others see the glass as half-empty, these individuals see it as half-full. While others fear the approaching darkness of night, these anticipate the dawn of morning. Clearly, mountains cannot be moved, but they can be climbed. Each struggle helped to form a reservoir of determination and resiliency. This would prove to be an invaluable asset in a world where the color of one's skin was the basis for defining one's place in the social order.

Much of our perception of self is determined by how we imagine we appear to others and how others react to us. The conclusions we draw about ourselves as a result of this assessment can have a profound affect on our emerging self-concept and self-esteem. The unique historical circumstances surrounding the African-American intro-duction into American culture provide a conceptual framework that clearly articulates the relevancy of what has been termed the "looking-glass-self" (Doob, 1988, p. 121).

The media bombards us with a daily plethora of depressing stories regarding the ills of inner-city life. We are fed a steady diet of the consequences of sociopathology gone awry. The daily newspapers seem to allocate a disproportionate amount of space to stories of black-on-black crime, high rates of illegitimacy for black teenagers and the virtual disintegration of the black family. The constant focus on such problems gives the impression that these problems are totally pervasive and typically associated with blacks. In this regard, the power of the media to socially construct reality is unparalleled. The persistent image on national TV of black males being carted off to jail for crimes against persons leaves an indelible mark on the psyche of the American viewer. Indubitably, it becomes the accepted image of most black males and blacks in general. Likewise, the persistent images of semiliterate young mothers on welfare and blacks living in the worst public housing projects in the city send similar messages.

The media exert a powerful impact on the formation of social attitudes among African-American youth (Leifer et al. 1974). Keller (1963) provides some clues as to the process whereby the media have been able to insinuate their image into the lives of lower-class youth. He concludes that because lower-class youth watch more television than other groups, television has become an influential force in the lives of these youths. Greenberg (1972) not only notes the high incidence of television viewing among African-American youth but also includes the impact of radio listening, noting that African-American youth, on average, engage in more television viewing and radio listening than other Americans.

The media, particularly television, are masterful purveyors of cultural norms, values and social attitudes. To the extent that the media portray certain groups in a less than desirable light, the media can also have a debilitating impact on the perception these groups have of themselves (Cartwright et al. 1975). The impact of this media-created image of a specific ethnic group is emotionally, psychologically, and socially debilitating for the victims as well as the general public, who watch television and tend to perpetuate racial divisiveness and fear. However, most devastating is the impact of such a media campaign on the very young children who must live out their daily existence in crime-infested environments. The media-created caricature of black Americans robs black children, in particular, of their most effective defense against the sociopathology that envelopes them—self-esteem and hope.

The historic and economic circumstances under which African-Americans were introduced into the culture made it necessary to ascribe them a lower status. This negative, ascribed status, at its most fundamental level, has been resistant to change and some would say exacerbated with the advent of the electronic media. The media blitz of negative images and social reality sends a clear message of hopelessness to those living the lifestyle. This is often exacerbated by the lack of positive role models in African-American communities and the failure of the media to promote such models. Submission evolves in the absence of hope.

While the visual and printed media have been perhaps the most visible purveyors of this image, the impact of the process has been no less deleterious as it is perpetuated by the dominant hegemony in the classroom, the boardroom, and manifested in social policy. Many would contend that the disproportionate representation of African-Americans among the ranks of the lower class are inextricably tied to this phenomenon. Over forty years after the landmark, *Brown vs. Board of Education of Topeka,* Kansas, case, busing is still an issue, and many urban and suburban classrooms have become resegregated. Despite laws against housing discrimination, African-Americans remain concentrated in certain areas of urban centers and suburbs and white flight continues. African-American males are disproportionately represented among the inmates in our penal institutions. These are the odds against which African Americans must struggle.

The preceding discourse colors the landscape that surrounds the stories. Its purpose is to clearly articulate the fact that the African-American lives in a different world from the dominant culture and is confronted with many issues based on race that are not part of the experience of the majority population. While sharing many common experiences with the dominant culture related to life transitions, the African-American carries the extra baggage of race.

The oral histories that are the subject of this book are stories of triumph. They are stories of the ability of ordinary people to do extraordinary things. Most important, they are stories that give voice to the multitude of people who in their private worlds struggle to triumph over adversity. They are stories that will hopefully provide a blueprint for change.

What about those who do not succumb? What about those who succeed against the odds and grow and develop into goal-oriented, successful adults? How is it that their lives took a different path? What is the spark that keeps hope alive for these individuals? What are the variables that insulate these individuals from the potential devastating effects of a socially ascribed, inferior status based on race and an often negative socially construed collective self-image? Why are some able to overcome adversity and others not? These are the questions that will be explored in this book.

The reader will enter into the lives of African-Americans who have struggled to overcome such problems as alcoholism, drug addiction, incest, learning disabilities, physical challenges, divorce, gangs, poverty, and racial identity. Through their oral histories, the reader will be in the unique position of viewing the world through the eyes of the other. This experience will be conscious raising, creating a foundation for understanding. It will take the reader to the first step toward shedding underlying assumptions about others and will view with increased acuity that which lies beyond his or her own personal experience.

Oral histories were recorded for the following sixteen African-American adults (nine males and seven females), who were reared or spent a major portion of their lives in the Chicago metropolitan area. Their biographical data include their first names, approximate age, occupation, and major life issue(s). To protect their anonymity, only first names are used. Similarly, some names and places may also have been changed:

Andrea is a woman in her late thirties, who works as a school social worker. She is divorced and struggled to raise a daughter as a single parent, while pursuing her college degree.

Carole is a vibrant, energetic woman in her early fifties. She is an entrepreneur who triumphed over the emotional scars of childhood sexual abuse.

Juanita is a soft-spoken, sensitive woman in her early forties. She is a teacher. Raised from age four in a foster home, she struggled to find love and a sense of belonging.

Ernestine is a widow in her late seventies. As a homemaker, she and her husband struggled to raise a large family with limited financial resources.

Joyce is a quiet, soft-spoken woman in her mid-fifties. She is a skilled hospital technician who also owns her own business. She is a divorced mother of two grown children and struggles with a learning disability.

Lorna is an assertive, outspoken woman in her early sixties. The divorced mother of two, she acquired a GED, bachelor's, and master's degrees while battling a serious illness, to become an adult education teacher.

Yolanda is a very shy college student in her twenties. Bound to a wheelchair as a result of cerebral palsy, she continues to pursue her college education and harbors great aspirations for the future.

Kangi is a sensitive, pensive, youthful-looking male in his early sixties. His is a story of the struggle to come to grips with a parent's bisexuality, loss of a beloved father, poverty, and drug abuse.

Gregory is in his forties and works as a counselor in a program for at-risk students at a community college. His is a story of a man made thoughtful by years of struggling to reconcile the conflict emanating from a strong self-concept nurtured by his parents in his youth and a society that responded in ways that consistently challenged his perception of self.

George W. Sr. is a man in his nineties, who, though physically challenged by the amputation of one leg, lives independently in a senior citizens home under the watchful eye of his two sons, who were interviewed at the same time. As an entrepreneur with limited resources, he raised six children (five of whom have college degrees), assuming total responsibility for raising his children after the death of his wife at a young age.

George W. Jr. is a retired elementary school assistant superintendent and the eldest son of George W. Sr. He is in his sixties. His is a story of the family's struggle to realize dreams despite their financial circumstance and the loss of their mother.

John is in his early sixties and the middle son of George W. Sr. He speaks to the success of his siblings in relation to family values.

Lanell is an amicable police officer and minister in his thirties. Reared in a large family, his is a story of parental love and strong values as the foundation on which the ability to conquer adversity is built.

Steve was the youngest of the storytellers, at age twenty-six. He is employed as an academic skills/transition adviser at a local community college. As an African-American of mixed racial ancestry, his is a story of the search for racial and cultural identity.

Edward is in his middle forties and holds a supervisory position for a transportation company. He is a community activist and projects a sense of altruism. Raised in a family torn by alcoholism, he finds a surrogate father who brings order and stability to his life.

Dave is in his fifties and works as a chief custodian. A lifelong learner, he is certified in a number of skills. He is a man who uses his Bible as a blueprint for living. Raised by his grandmother in the rural South, his is a story of triumph over poverty.

Only seven of the recorded oral histories will be presented in their entirety. These were selected as their stories more clearly illustrate the connection between the interpretation of social reality and success in conquering adversity. The remaining nine will be presented in excerpted form to support the recurring themes. To maintain the authenticity of the oral histories, the dialects of the storytellers were preserved. Additionally, the reader may encounter some repetition, as excerpts from the seven oral histories presented in their entirety may also be used elsewhere.

Chapters 2 through 8 consist of the oral histories of Kangi, Joyce, Steve, Juanita, Gregory, Carole and Edward and are presented in their entirety. Each storyteller was asked the question, "If you had to name your story, what would you call it?" For the most part, it was from their answer to this question that the chapter title for their life history was born. Other chapter titles emerged from the life philosophy extracted from the life history as told by the storyteller.

While each storyteller's experiences were unique, the fabric of each of their stories is woven together by some common threads. Chapters 9 through 12 consist of a discussion of the four primary themes that emerged from the oral histories. Each chapter deals with one of the themes and its subcategories. The four themes are stated metaphorically as the title of each chapter, which are:

On Solid Ground I Stand: Family Roots—This chapter examines the socialization process with an emphasis on values clarification, strong work ethic, positive parental role models, discipline, consistent parental response, responsibility, accountability, and sacrifice. It elucidates the role of these variables in the formation of personality traits that assisted the storytellers in confronting adversity.

It Takes a Village to Raise a Child: Support Systems—Here such variables as significant others, mentors, effective teachers, community cohesiveness, and the partnership between home, school, and community are explored. This chapter emphasizes the importance of support systems as a factor in triumph over adversity.

Light a Candle and Curse the Darkness: Resistance—The significance of race perception, self-esteem, the value of negative experiences, and goal-setting are the major focuses of this chapter. It explores the significance of resistance as a motivating force behind the drive to defy external or socially constructed definitions of self.

Faith Can Move Mountains: Spirituality—Here the role of strong religious conviction is explored as it impacts persistence, perseverance, and determination in conquering adversity.

Chapter 13 presents the summary of the data from recurring themes, conclusions, implications for education and the African-American family and community.

Whether or not the ability to surmount personal struggles can be directly attributed to these common variables is left to the reader to draw the final conclusion. However, one cannot ignore the significance of these variables in the lives of the storytellers.

And now, our journey begins.

2

Long Journey Home: Kangi's Story

Kangi is a youthful looking African-American male in his early sixties. He projects a very serious businesslike demeanor that softens upon getting to know him. He is a very sensitive individual who, by his own admission, has always been an advocate for the less fortunate. His is a story of a struggle to come to grips with a parent's bisexuality, the loss of a beloved father at an early age, poverty, alcohol, and drug abuse.

My parents were from the rural South, and I was one of eight children. When I was born three of my siblings had previously passed. My dad was a mucker in the mines of Alabama; my mother was a housewife. I was born October 3, 1932, in Alabama. At the age of six months, we moved to Chicago. My father preceded us there. He got a job, then sent for us.

My parents relocated from the South for economic reasons. Work was very very light in the South. The economic conditions were very poor and also the social conditions were poor. My mother's sister had preceded us to Chicago, and I was told most black people who were impoverished, felt Chicago was like the promised land. So that was why they came to Chicago.

My dad encouraged discipline and respect. He was a family man. We did things together and his idea was church being first. We could never go to the show or anyplace until we had been to church on Sunday. My father was an usher at Progressive Baptist Church; I never will forget that. We were very religious oriented. I remember on Sunday mornings listening to Wings Over Jordan, a gospel group out of Tuskegee. As we listened, mama would comb our hair and what-have-you. We all went to church together. We went to Progressive up until the time he passed. We had a very strong base.

From a discipline standpoint, if dad was at work and we were acting up, my mother would say "I'm going to tell your dad." "Rigomortis" would set in, because he didn't whip you, he'd beat you. He never touched my sister, because when he whipped you, it would last you a long time. He just didn't take no stuff. Yet, we loved our dad. The only person that didn't love him was my oldest brother Ralph. Ralph was homosexual. To my knowledge, he never had a girlfriend and my dad could not understand it. My dad took us to ball games. At that time, it was the old Negro League on 35th. My brother would say, "I don't want to go, because I don't like baseball." And my dad would say things like "All boys like baseball. What do you mean you don't like baseball?" POW! (as in physically strike him). He'd beat my brother, because he jumped double dutch, played hopscotch and jacks. He was just effeminate. My dad just didn't know how to deal with it. Neither did my mother, because they didn't know anything about that. My mother drew my brother closer to her to protect him, instead of seeking some help. My brother died very young. He had a massive heart attack, at the age of 36. My father died at 38. Otherwise, I would say my relationship with my parents was good, until the later years.

As far as family activities, what could you do, having just enough money to get by. When my dad was living, we'd take rides on the L on Sundays. Everybody'd dress up, and ride the L downtown. That was great. We'd go to Washington Park, for a family picnic and on holidays; I loved it.

My dad was an excellent cook. He would cook all the family meals. In fact the day he died, he had cooked that Thanksgiving meal. He could really cook. I always imagined him as like a superman. I don't know why he did all these things, because mother could cook, but he just did it. Southern women, at that time, were dominated by their males. The woman just stayed at home. She just took care of the kids. She didn't go out and do anything. I guess that's why mama never rebelled. Then, when he died, she let it all hang out. My mother liked to dance. She was lively. In fact, that was the hardest part when she got ill. She had been so active in her life, to see her like that, it devastated me.

My father actually dropped dead in 1941. We were having Thanksgiving dinner, and he got sick at the table. I told my mother, "Something's wrong with Dad, I think he's dying." I actually spoke those words. My mother said, "Boy shut your mouth." So my dad said he didn't feel good, and he went and laid down. Then we heard a noise. We went to the bedroom and he wasn't there, we went to the washroom and he had fallen to the floor.

I was nine at that time, and I was very close to my father. I was like his pick, because I was very athletic. My dad liked sports and I did too. I'll never forget that day because we had an old fashion commode at that time. It was a pipe with the flush box at the top. When my dad fell, he pulled that pipe out of the wall and the commode pulled up

out of the concrete. He was lying in the water and I'll never forget
that froth at his mouth. We ran, of course, and they called the fire
department and police, and they took him out. My mother came back
and said, "Your dad is not coming back anymore." It was quite a
heartbreaking situation. At that time there were 5 children; Ralph was
the oldest at eleven, I was nine and Fred, Vernon and Carol were after
me.

I liked the idea of him providing, because I understand that he had
been sick quite some time. But he didn't want to take days off
because he knew he needed the money for us. He was a man who
loved his family and I always felt that. I have a lot of respect for men
that will take care of their families. Guys tell me about getting over
on their wives, don't take care bills, don't take care of their family, I
don't even want to talk to you. Any man that doesn't take care of his
family is somebody I don't want to deal with. So that was one value I
got in my head that way.

Our strong base deteriorated somewhat after my father passed. My
mother had never worked. She knew nothing about work. My dad
did all the shopping for groceries and everything. All my mother did
was care for us. Therefore, my mother was in utter chaos after my
father died. She didn't know what she would do. I had several aunts
and uncles who lived in the South, but Aunt Mabel and Aunt June
lived in Chicago. They told my mother, "We'll take a kid" and my
mother said, "No, I'll not let you take my children. If you want to
help me with them, fine, but I'm not going to give my kids away."
That's why I became very familiar with what is now considered Aid for
Dependent Children.

We received a check once a month. I think the whole sum was
about $158 for the five kids at that time. We lived in a basement
apartment and the rent was $40. I remember $40 a month, and the
reason I remember the amount is because I began to complain about
not getting shoes and clothes. I told my mother, "I want my own
check," because this check used to come, written Kangi, son of
Frances. I said, "I want my check." One day mama said, "Let me
show you the budget." She sat me down and showed me how the
money was broken down. The rent was $40 for five rooms.

Still, my upbringing was pretty happy. We had a happy time,
because we had a good mother. We had a lot of fun together, but it
was very very hard times. I remember waking up at night and rats
were actually in the bed with me and I could see in the morning where
their footprints had been all around my head. I would go in the
kitchen and rats would jump out of the stove. It was as if the rats felt
they lived there. You couldn't scare them away.

I remember very vividly taking a bath once a week because we had
to heat the water. Heating up water to take a bath takes a lot of water.
I remember mama washing clothes on a washboard or sending the

clothes to what we called wet wash. They'd come back washed and you had to hang them out to dry, then mama would have to iron them. You can imagine that for five kids. I remember sharing clothes, because we were on aid and a lot of times my brother would wear a coat one day and I'd wear it the next. Mama took turns buying us clothes, because of the financial situation, but we managed to survive pretty well.

I was very good in school. Athletically, I played ball. I was so wrapped up between school and ball that a lot of things around me I wasn't even aware of. We had some strange meals, like sugar and butter sandwiches. Mama made butter. We were on "chairdy." They called it "chairdy" and we would get this milk. They would give it to us and mama would let it clabber, and we had a churn and she would churn and actually make butter in the house. We didn't have a refrigerator; we had what you call an ice box. We'd buy about seventy-five pounds of ice from the ice man, and we'd put it in there. Once it melted, of course, everything would spoil. So, you didn't have leftovers. I actually remember mama using a wood stove. We'd have wood to cook with in the house until we finally got gas.

I can't remember when we got a phone, because a phone was a luxury. If you were on aid and got a phone, the workers would come and say, "You're doing too well, maybe you don't need to be on aid." I remember my mother actually told them, she didn't want to deal with them anymore, because the neighbors would spy on you and tell the aid worker how we were living. Mama kept us so clean and neat, even though we had rags, they seemed to think we had some other income. Finally, my mother told the worker one day "Look, I don't want to hear no more questions, just get out. You all don't send us no more money. We'll make it." Eventually, mama got a job working in the war, as a riveter. Following that, she began to work as a nurse's aide.

We were really raised by people in the neighborhood. Some of the gangs (they had gangs then) would steal food. We'd wake up in the morning, at our basement apartment, and they would have dumped bushel baskets of greens and firewood. The gangs took care of us. They would steal and give it to us; they were kids a little older than me. They were teenagers who knew my father had died, and they told my mother, "We'll take care of you all." They actually did this. They would steal ice or anything they thought we needed. If they were on the corner cursing, when they'd see my mother, they all called her Ma, and they'd stop. We had gangs then, but in my neighborhood the kids really respected older people. Any parent on the street could chastise you, and you "yes sir" and "yes ma'am" them, and we kept our street clean.

There was a lady across the street, I never will forget, we would sweep the street, and she would pay us to keep them clean. We would earn money by cutting kindling wood, because most people did not have gas heat then. We had pot-bellied stoves or either kerosene stoves to keep warm and that was one of my chores, to make the fire.

My dad and I had a good relationship. But after my dad passed, I found out my father was very abusive to my mother. She told me some things, because I worshipped him. So, she wanted to straighten me out, to let me know my dad wasn't such a God. As I grew older, I found out what my mother was too. My mother was bisexual and after my father died, she just threw caution to the wind.

My mother chose not to ever remarry, I guess because of my sister. We had one sister, Carol. It turned out it was a wise move, but then again, it wasn't such a wise move in a way because my sister married. She quit high school and got married. My mother claimed that's why she didn't remarry, but it turned out my mother had switched. She lost all affection for men basically.

The neighborhood was aware of my mother's sexual orientation. There were other women in the neighborhood like that, my mother hung out with. Then we started going to this church. The lady that took us there lived in the back. Her mother used to babysit for us. She was the first lady I was really aware was close to my mother. We started going to that church. Even today, that church is predominantly attended by people of "that" persuasion.

I found out later, the reason my sister got married was to get out of the house, because the women my mother was consorting with began to bother my sister. It caused my brother Vernon some very serious problems. Until about two years ago, he would tell you quickly he hated my mother. I didn't see any of it, because I was into school, my books and my athletics.

My mother was the type of lady who liked to party. She went to church, but she was a very popular lady in the neighborhood. She had a lot of boyfriends, guys would want to marry her, but when they saw five kids, and ma would always tell them, no it's a package deal, people would say, "I'll marry you, you get rid of the kids." If a guy took anytime with my mother, he had to have money. One friend my mother had, let all of us work in his grocery store after school. So naturally, we were able to eat pretty good. My mother did anything that would get money. She was a judge for years. She worked at the polling place and that was additional money and kept food on the table for us. She was good at that. Any way there was to get some money, mom would get it, to take care of us kids so we could make it.

One of the values my mother taught us, and my dad too even before he passed, you work for whatever you get. I see kids today hustling on the streets begging for cans. My dad had us go out getting junk or going to the store for people. Whatever we did, we had to earn what we got. Mama taught us how to look out for each other and to keep family business among ourselves. Dad would tell us if you get into a fight, do whatever you have to do, with the help of your brothers, to win, to take care of the family member. If the police get involved, I'll take care of it. So those were some values that we got and we're like that today. In spite of my mother's weakness for that thing, she taught me that a single woman can raise kids, and I think we came out pretty good. Mama pushed in spite of difficulties. It was all she could do. I remember when I finished high school, she said, " I can't go no further with you."

My mother, of course, disciplined us after my father passed, and she could be pretty tough too. I had occasion to get very angry at my sister because I had to do what I thought only girls should do. We had to mop the floor, wash dishes, empty garbage. So, I remember mopping the floor one night, hurrying up because mama was coming home from work and the babysitter left and I hadn't done it. So, I'm trying to hurry up and get it done and there were two bunk beds, Carol slept at the top and Vernon slept at the bottom. Carol was saying, "Yeah, yeah, yeah, you got to mop the floor, you got to mop the floor." I came back and popped her in the nose. She bled; blood went everywhere. So mama came home. Carol said, "He hit me in the nose." My mother just said, "Uummm." She didn't do anything for about three days.

I was playing ball one day, I got through playing ball, the children had left the house doing something. My mother called me in the front room. She said, "Hey, I want to talk to you, little guy." So, I came in. She said, "You like to hit girls in the nose, huh. Well, I'm going to hit you in your face." My mother took an iron cord and doubled it about three times, and she hit me in my face, I don't know how many times. My face swelled up, you would have thought I'd been attacked by a horde of bumble bees. She would hit you with a garbage can top. I remember my brother had to empty the garbage one night because he hadn't done it. He looked backed and she just took the top of the garbage can and right on the top of his head, BAM. She would throw a fork at you. She'd make you get on your knees by the bed and take a strap to you. But for the most part, I thought we were pretty disciplined kids. Mama told us to be home at 9 o'clock. When it got dark you can believe everybody was sitting on that porch at 9 o'clock. I don't care where mama was. You knew when it started getting dark you'd better get it home.

We felt it was our parents' responsibility to discipline us. This was what they were supposed to do; so we accepted it. Kids in the neighborhood used to laugh about the beatings we got. A guy lived behind us named Lester Willis; we used to listen at the wall when he got his beating, and we'd laugh about it. But no problem, nobody was calling the police talking about brutality. Parents disciplined kids, and that was just it. We accepted it, no problem. There was never any expression of animosity toward our parents, as far as discipline was concerned. We were frightened of my dad in that sense, but we weren't scared of him. If we did wrong, we knew what he was going to do.

I don't recall a lot of show of affection. It seemed my parents' total concern was food, keeping our clothes clean. Mama worked so hard. Can you imagine washing clothes for five kids on your hands, ironing piece by piece, getting us to school, that kind of thing? Affection mostly came in terms of expression. My dad just worked. He worked himself to death, literally.

My oldest brother, Ralph, didn't like my dad at all, because of that problem. I remember my brother saying he was going to urinate on dad's grave. He couldn't stand my father, but you wouldn't either, if somebody slapped you in the face and abused you like that. Dad just couldn't understand how Ralph could be that way. Being an ignorant man, he didn't know. That was a rough part of my upbringing. I was in denial, to a point. Once my father died, there was my mother and my brother Ralph. I always felt I had to prove to the whole neighborhood that I wasn't like that. That was a problem.

I didn't try to prove myself, until I got older. Before that, as far as girls were concern, I couldn't care less because all I wanted was to play ball. I was a "booky" (as in bookworm). They used to call me "The Book." I'd read anything and everything, even in high school. I had one girlfriend and she's dead now; that's the only girl I thought I really liked, Rosemary. But otherwise, it was ball.

As I grew up, I started liking girls. At the same time, they never could get close to me. I had a difficult time with that. The only thing I felt a woman was, in terms of a relationship with a guy, was to prove that I wasn't funny. I couldn't develop any type of commitment. It was something I couldn't do. I struggled with that. It's very difficult for me to give myself to others, until I was forty-five years old, when I married my wife. She understood me, and we worked through that. I got therapy for that, not from a psychiatrist, but through church, small group ministry, where that came out.

I just didn't want to be classified. I went to a church and people used to say, you go to that kind of church you must be funny too. Your ma and your brother are that way. That was rough and that's why I have a lot of compassion and empathy for people like that, because you don't know why people are the way they are. You jump to conclusion, you don't know. That's why I minister to people of different lifestyles. It has been so effective because I've been there. I had to come through it myself.

The neighborhood was tight to the point that if anybody had any type of calamity, the neighborhood came to their aid. We shared food stamps, if you will, our rations. We really took care of each other. Still the gangs had their little warfares but not like today. They didn't deal with drugs. It was just their turf. It was like a club, but it had a little violence. Every now and then, somebody would shoot somebody over a girl or something like that, but it wasn't like it is today. They had colors and you knew if you wandered into another neighborhood, you might get a whipping, but you wouldn't get shot. They'd just jump on you and beat you up. There were the Gay Lords, the Counts, the Deacons and The Four Corners. We were the Czars. I never belonged to a gang. I was always athletic. I was a good ballplayer, and they knew me by that, Peewee, Joe Louis.

I used to fight. I was good. I could fight and that was why I got the name Joe Louis. I would fight in a minute and a lot of times I got in fights because of my brother. Call my brother a sissy and I would take up. I had a vicious temper and I'd fight. I played shortstop in baseball. In fact, I felt that if the was timing right, I probably could have went to the Major Leagues. I played good. I could run like a deer. When you're an athlete, the gangs don't mess with you. They call you by that and they don't mess with you. So, I transcended the gangs. A lot of guys I played ball with were in the gang, but they were about two, three, four years older than me. I just played up to their level. So, I escaped the gangs.

Our community was all black at that time. There was a Mason-Dixon Line. If you crossed Drexel that was white. The only thing you could cross Drexel to do was to shop. When it got dark in Chicago you came back. From six months until I was eighteen, I lived on Evans in that basement apartment. Basically, people were poor. I don't know what the median income was at the time, but we were poor, yet happy.

To tell you the truth, being poor was no problem. The only thing I would sense, was when I walked to Du Sable High School (all the way from 43rd and Evans to 49th), I wore gym shoes with cardboard in the bottom. I was sensitive to that. I remember the couch where we had a tin can holding it up, and all the rats. It would be so cold, sometimes, and we couldn't afford coal in the winter, so we all slept in our clothes. You accept it as normal. You got used to it, so you didn't complain.

Racial equality was not a consideration then. We didn't look at that, honestly. We were not made as aware, because television didn't come until 1947 or '48. A lot of the exposure through the media to racial divisiveness was not with us. We knew that white people lived over there and we lived over here, but as to how they felt about us, it wasn't a concern. I just knew that because they were white and I was black, I lived over here and they lived over there. As far as them thinking they were better than me or me thinking I was less, I always felt equal, in terms of my intelligence, and nobody poisoned my mind. Nobody ever told me anything different. Oh, we'd call them "Ofays" or "grays."

The only real social contact I had was playing ball, and we'd always beat them badly. We were good. I went over in the Stock Yards, over on Damon, I played all over and had no problems. Even when I got to high school, we played against Kelly High School, Lindbloom High School, Tilden High School, and they were all white, and we got along with them. So, the attitude was a little different. That's why I didn't feel I was at a disadvantage. I felt the opportunities would come for me, because I was qualified. There was no reason to think there was a problem, although that wasn't necessarily the case.

I think most of us, in my neighborhood, felt that way. We had our world, they had theirs. You just didn't interact. So, you didn't know what was going on. You knew they had the better jobs. All the streetcar motormen were white, the police were white. If you went to the bank, you knew everybody was white. They had the better jobs, but you just accepted it as, this is the way it is.

The only time we were really aware of it and we joke about it because there was a white gang called the Basement Street Boys, if they'd catch you, they'd do something to you. By the same token, if anybody white crossed our territory and got caught over there at night, something might happen to them too. As far as white people were concerned, the ones we dealt with more than anything else were Jews who had stores in our community. The groceries and the commodities like socks and stockings, and we got along with them. We knew what they were about, because we worked for them.

I worked for a Jewish guy who had a grocery store. He always wanted to give me groceries and I told him, "I don't want groceries. I want money." They'd always want to give you something. It was that kind of thing. They didn't want to pay you what you were really worth. They were always trying to show you that, you didn't need as much money. I sensed that at an early age, but I have no prejudice against them.

My only other dealing with white people was when I went downtown. In my neighborhood, you never saw them, except maybe like an insurance man, or they would make deliveries. The police, one particular squad car 162, were white. We had no black policemen when I grew up and if they did, they were only in black neighborhoods. There was Two-Gun Pete and Indian Joe.

Two-Gun Pete and Indian Joe were black. They were well known. In fact, there was a series of articles on them in *Ebony*. Two-Gun Pete killed a lot of black men. He was known to carry a lot of guns, and he would kill people real quick. Black people didn't like him; they were real frightened by him.

I remember when I first started going to the poolroom. I thought that was great. I used to stand outside the window and watch these guys play pool. So, I put my age up. I got a draft card, because you had to have a draft card to go in the poolroom. There were a lot of guys shooting dope, even when I was growing up. The predominant drug was marijuana and heroin. A lot of guys were shooting needles;

a lot of my friends were shooting needles in their arms. The guy that owned the poolroom would say, "Two-Gun Pete's on his way. All you dope addicts better get out of here." I mean, they feared him. There were stories about him at school. He would arrest guys and tell them he didn't have time to take them to the police station, tell them to go and arrest themselves and he'll come down, and they did it. This man was something. He was violent. He would catch you shooting dice and come up and kick you in the face. He was really violent. He abused a lot of young black men, but he died a natural death. He's a legend on the south side of Chicago. It's a wonder somebody didn't kill him. But, nobody ever really tried to do anything to the police then. The police were very brutal and kicked your door down. You just didn't have any rights. When the police came, everybody just backed up. They'd just come right in, and all of them were big white Irishmen. They came in like gangbusters and you backed up. That was it. It was strictly black and poor people, so we suffered.

Then when the Civil Rights Movement came in, you became aware of how deprived you were of your rights. I became aware of it during summers. Mama would send us South, and they had the white fountains and the colored fountains. They moved you on the train. You get on the train, and if you were going South, when you got to a certain location, they would switch the cars so all the black people would be in the back of the train. Then later on, they just put you in a car in Chicago; that way you didn't have to move. You didn't know what was happening, but you didn't see any white people in the car with you. Racism didn't really affect me until I got in the military. That was my first real experience.

Of all my family, I was the most studious and I was encouraged in academics, although my mother only finished junior high. My dad had little or no education. He was almost illiterate. But mama pushed me in school as far as she could. I was a "booky." It looked like I was born reading. I was reading at an eighth-grade level in fourth grade. They selected me to go to the Lab School at the University of Chicago out of Forestville School which in 1946 was in a very poor neighborhood. So, I was encouraged educationally.

I wanted to be a lawyer, and everybody thought I would be. My mother was just sure I would accomplish anything educationally. My mother named all of us after famous people. She tried to do that. I don't know if that had anything to do with it or not. I can't recall if anybody in my family was well educated. I had one cousin who was an optometrist. He may have been somewhat of an influence on me.

Then there was a lady minister who encouraged me a lot. Her nickname was Snooky; her real name was Rev. Lillian Logan. She had a junk shop, a resale shop on 43rd and State, and I used to go there and sit with her for hours and she would encourage me. Another lady down the street named Mrs. Stanton, I helped put her son through high school, because I did all of his tests. He was lazy. He was crazy about me. He's dead now too. But, I did all his homework. I could do it and all the kids looked to me for that. That might have encouraged me. I liked the attention, because I could always do it.

I was the first one in my family who seemed to get into academics. They just did the best they could. As I said, my dad didn't have it, my mom didn't have it. In fact, I was going to write my life story once. I'll never forget. I wrote "My mother wasn't nothing, my dad wasn't nothing and nothing from nothing leaves nothing." My mother saw it and she said, "What are you, are you crazy? You must be out of your mind. Are you nuts?" Education, they didn't have and my mother was real frightened. She was a country woman, very conservative. She wasn't adventurous. She lived in a very small world.

My experiences in school were excellent in spite of the fact that we were on the "chairdy." The kids laughed at us because of the clothes we wore, and a lot of them had fathers and wore a little better clothes. But, I had some very good experiences.

I guess the teacher that impressed me most was my kindergarten teacher. I'll never forget her. Her name was Miss Bixby. I can remember that clearly. Miss Bixby was white and she was special, because she acted like a little child. I loved her. Then there was my first grade teacher, Miss Smith. Teachers liked me because I was a smart kid. The only time I had any trouble in terms of discipline in school was in 4th grade. There was a teacher named Miss Lacy. She was such a strong disciplinarian, and I always liked to make jokes. I was always a practical joker and I got in trouble for that, putting girls' hair in ink wells, putting thumb tacks in people's seats. I'd do all kinds of little devilish things. I liked to make people laugh, but I was always good. My last year in grammar school (I graduated a year ahead of time), I had Miss Thompkins who was a writer for the *Chicago Daily Defender*. She was a pianist and she wrote music. She was a very elegant lady. She was African-American. I only had one white teacher in grammar school and that was the one in kindergarten. After that, all my teachers were black. They were excellent teachers. They really loved the children. If somebody responds to you, you're going to give your best. There were no discipline problems in my school. As far as any dropouts and truancy, there was very very little because of the parents. Kids came to school.

We had families. Most of the kids I went to school with had mothers and fathers, so that meant kids were more stable. It wasn't that big scuffle. If anybody had wanted to ditch it should have been us, because we were always scuffling, in the sense of just getting enough to eat or clothes to wear. I remember when I graduated, I didn't know whether I was going to have a suit to wear. I think Aunt June bought my shoes and maybe Aunt Mabel bought me a suit. They had to really scuffle to get me out of there. I had no extra anything.

The worse time was the graduation, because I couldn't go to anything. I came home after the graduation. Everybody else had little parties to go to. I got a class ring and I gave that to a girl, with my dumb self. My mother scuffled to get that ring. I think at that time, the ring was $21. I got the ring, but I didn't go to the prom. I couldn't go to that. I had no extra anything. I had a nice suit and that was the end.

But, I just loved school. I loved everything about it, the homework. I had no problems with it at all. I can't speak for my brothers and sisters, but school was really an exciting time for me. I just wasn't in the "in crowd," because I didn't have the clothes. I was never socially accepted. But in terms of my athletics, now that was different. A lot of kids had jobs, and their parents had a little more. My mother did the best she could up to that point.

Then, I went on to high school. Because I graduated a year ahead, perhaps that hurt me from a social standpoint. I didn't adjust well when I first went, because I had skipped a grade. So, I went to Du Sable High School in 1946. I took general courses, I didn't take anything difficult. I didn't know to take anything difficult.

Basically, all of my teachers were African-American. I had good experiences even with the white teachers that were there. My geometry teacher, Mr. Patton, was African-American and I'll never forget him, because he wasn't going to let me graduate. He told me the first day in class, "Kangi, you got straight S's under Miss Farris, I expect no less than an S." I said, "That's not fair. I may not be able to get it." He said, "If you do that, if you don't get it, you'll be doing less than you're capable of doing and I'm going to fail you. Either you're going to get all 'S's' or you're going to fail." And I failed.

I just wouldn't do it. We had twenty-six propositions to do, and I just couldn't handle it. I don't know, I forgot all my propositions, I forgot equations, all the rules of geometry. So, I cut. I couldn't go. I ended up having to go to summer school, otherwise I wouldn't have graduated. You know who I took in summer school? I took Miss Farris. She wasn't going to flunk me. I got through it. High school was a lot of fun, but at the same time, it was the same old story. I remember having to wash the same shirt over and over. I didn't have the clothes. Half the time, I couldn't eat lunch. They had boosters, dances on Friday, I couldn't go to anything. A lot of kids had jobs. I just didn't have it, but I wouldn't miss school. I just loved school, but all the extra-curricula activities, like going to basketball games and football games, it was rare for me to be able to go. We just didn't have the money.

It didn't sadden me, because the joy for me was playing ball. I cannot underestimate it. I was a tremendous ballplayer and I played in front of big huge crowds of people. I played all over the City of Chicago. I was known. That was the thing that kept me going. One thing that hurt me real bad was when I was the bat boy for a team. They played for money and they worked all year. These were men, old men and they bought these beautiful uniforms, jackets and everything. They gave me one and my mother made me quit, because they played most of their games on Sunday and I had to go to church, and mama made me quit. I had to give the uniform back. Oh that hurt me. I had this nice jacket, it was sharp. The uniform wasn't silk, but it was good stuff and they had bought me everything, spikes. I had everything, and I had to give it up. Mama said, "You got to go to church," and I did. I'll never forget that. But that was what took me through. I'd leave school, come home and play ball and that got me over. I just didn't see the poverty.

People ask why I didn't get into professional baseball. Well, at that time, the only black school that had a baseball team was Phillips and I went to Du Sable. We didn't have a baseball team. They had black baseball players, games in the park, but I didn't get into it. I didn't play baseball until I went into the service, and I guess it was a little late for me then. I had one tryout. The White Sox had a tryout at Jackson Park, 63rd and Stony Island; I went one day and I didn't have a good experience. I couldn't hit a curve ball or something like that. Nobody really pushed me in that way. As much as they talked about it, I didn't have the mentors, somebody that would really encourage me.

In high school, my teachers were good, they really were. The teachers were really dedicated. I don't know where the idea that teachers didn't care came in in later years, where people were just making money. You have to understand, during the time I came up, to be a teacher, particularly a black teacher, was an honored profession. Teachers are not honored today like they were then. I mean teachers were really thought of highly. To be a schoolteacher, my goodness, you were somebody. We just respected a person that was teaching us, and the kids responded.

The neighbors thought a lot of me, because I was smart. I remember going to college and everybody donated money for my car fare. In fact, the church I went to paid my tuition for the first year. They bought books for me, but it was just other things, social things that I couldn't keep up with. So, I just gave up. I dropped out and went into what they call United States Air Force Institute to finish my education, but other things happened that waylaid my education.

My first assignment was Wichita Falls, Texas, no racism. I was known as Little Kangi from Chicago; I had it on my cap. White guys took care of me. Once again, playing ball, and I boxed too. I was a prize fighter and most of the guys were from Chicago, New York and the like. Blacks, particularly, were respected by the white guys. They thought we were gangsters. I went to Wichita Falls, Texas, for school. Still no problem, because I never went to town. In basic training, you weren't allowed to go to town. After that, they shipped me to Denver, Colorado, to school and that was my first experience with racism.

There were two black guys in my outfit in Denver. This white guy played his hillbilly music all the time, LOUD! I turned his radio down and said, "Hey, man that stuff's too loud." He and I fought (I thought I could still fight), and he broke my nose. My buddy Edgar, who is black, shocked him. I'll never forget, he pulled a switchblade on this white guy and said, "Man if you ever do anything to Kangi again I'll cut your throat." The white guy told me, "You never did anything to me, really man, but I just hate black people. I been taught that from a kid." That was the first and only incident. I got through that.

When I finished school in Denver, they let us pick places we wanted to go for our assignment. I wanted to go overseas. I wanted to go to Germany, Europe and they sent me to Biloxi, Mississippi. I almost went crazy. I'd never been South, other than when I was a kid experiencing the two water fountains but nothing major. It didn't really have an impact on me. I said, Biloxi, Mississippi. How could I get that. I almost went crazy. So I went home; they gave me a little longer than nine days leave. I went home, and I told ma, "I'm not going." She said, "What do you mean you're not going. You got to go where they send you." I said, "No ma, I can't go to Mississippi because you heard the most terrible things about Mississippi." It was terrible. So, I went.

Now, I'm in Biloxi, Mississippi, I'm getting along pretty cool. In town, they had all the black people in one part of town, white people in the other. I didn't have any dealing with white people too much but at the same time, I knew where I was. This particular day, I'm in the barracks. All the guys from Chicago and New York stayed up in the top bunk. I'm still playing ball, by the way. I'm playing shortstop and the white boys were really scared of us. We wouldn't even let them come upstairs. We had one white guy up there from California and he talked like a brother. Otherwise, the hillbillies stayed downstairs. If they came up the steps, we'd run them down.

This black guy came in one day crying. He was from Brownsville, Texas, I'll never forget it. He was crying, I said, "Man what are you crying about?" He said, "They wouldn't cut my hair." I said to him, "What do you mean they wouldn't cut your hair. Where were you?. You know you're in Mississippi, man. You can't go in town, ask them white people to cut your hair." He said, "I was on the base." I said, "Naw, you wasn't, on the base? Ain't no discrimination in the military. They got to cut your hair. Where did you go?" I didn't even know they had a barbershop on the base.

When I got my hair cut, there were black and white guys getting their hair cut, but all the barbers were black. I didn't think anything about it. It turns out that there was a barbershop on the other side of the base, gorgeous. I mean like something out of New York; it had manicurist, ALL WHITE. I was always militant. So I said, "Oh, they won't cut your hair. Let's go." We went over there. We walked in, the lady said, "What you boys want?" I said, "What do you mean, what you boys want. We're airmen. What do you think we want. This is a barbershop, isn't it. It's obvious by our presence, we want haircuts." She said, "Well, I'm sorry, we don't cut no colored airmen's hair in here." I said, "You're going to either cut hair today or you're going to close it." I said, "Let me talk to whose in charge." She called the man. He came and I said, "What's this business about you not cutting colored hair. I understand we're in Mississippi, but what do you mean you're not going to cut our hair. I'm going to close this barbershop or you're going to cut our hair here. You're working on a military base, Truman signed a federal order." He said, "We ain't gonna cut no colored airman's hair, we'll quit." I said, "Well you're going to quit". I started my stuff. I went to my First Sergeant and he said, "You're crazy, little guy, you got a lot of guts."

What they did to me is really funny. I got all the guys riled up, and I got a call the next day, the chaplain who was black, Lt. Kent, I will never forget him, called me to his office. "Huh, what you doing?" I said, "What do you mean what am I doing?" He said, "What are you trying to do?" I said, "I'm not doing anything. I'm just trying to get what we got coming. We're going to start a protest. We're going to picket." He said, "Kangi, don't do that. We can work it out." I said, "Naw, you're a chaplain. I don't want to talk to you. You're God's man. You can't use the method we're going to use." He said, "I wish you wouldn't raise all this ruckus. Maybe we can work this out." I said, "No sir, Lt. Kent. I appreciate talking to you, but we're going to do something." Before it came to a head, do you know what happened to me? They shipped me out. I got orders.

To show you what they did to me, normally when you go overseas, they give you thirty days leave to be with your family. They gave me nine days. I had nine days to leave Mississippi, get to Chicago and then go all the way out to Camp Stoman, California, and I was going to be gone overseas for three years and six months. That was my first dealing with racism. Then, the word was out, if I came to town, they were going to do something to me. It was like that in 1950. That was when the orders started to integrate the military. Otherwise, I had no trouble with white guys. They stayed downstairs, we stayed upstairs. We wouldn't let them come upstairs. We used to start trouble with them.

They had two service clubs. These white guys had vans, and they would bring girls out for them, these hostesses. We'd go over there deliberately, and if a white guy got up, we'd sit down next to a white girl, and they would get RED. The white girls wouldn't dance with us, but we were over there. We were low down. We wanted to get it on, but we never had any fights, no riots on the base or nothing. The quarters were equal. It was just, the tension was there.

You're in the heart of Biloxi, Mississippi. As long as you're on the base, you were cool. I stayed down there nine months and I worked. I was a stock control specialist. I worked with white people, never had any problems on the base. They treated me with respect, I treated them with respect. If we were in town, that was another issue, if you got caught somewhere. That was the only experience of racism I had in the military except when I came from overseas.

Overseas, there was no racism, other than the fact that they tried to prejudice a lot of the Japanese against us. There were places where you'd find all whites and all blacks, but it's natural you'd want to be around your people unless you're in a situation where you had to mix.

I had a situation where, she wasn't a girlfriend, she was just a street girl and we were friends because I befriended all of the junkies. I always have been that way. I like strays. We were drinking beer one night, and I was the only black in there, and the Japanese girls were talking in Japanese. I didn't understand what they were saying. The girl I was with said, "They're talking about us." It was all white sailors in there, and it was about two blocks from base, I never will forget this because she said, "I'm going to make some trouble, Kangi." I said, "What kind of trouble are you going to make?" She said, "I make trouble." I said, "Don't make no trouble. It's about fifty of those guys, they'll kill me." She said, "I make trouble." She took this beer bottle, broke it, jumped up and charged toward these girls.

I hit that door running. She saw me two days later and said, "You chicken." I said, "You're crazy. You must be nuts." This was in Japan. There were Japanese girls who liked white guys and some Japanese girls liked black guys. Basically, there was no problem.

When I got in the service, I went crazy. I got off into drugs. In fact, I got busted for dealing drugs in the military, although I wasn't doing it, they just thought I was because I handled so much drugs. I was using it but not heavy enough to need it, so I'd give it to people. When the military police busted me, they arrested me. I stayed in jail three days. They kept me under confinement, where they had other addicts, to see how I'd react. I didn't need anything, but they were giving guys substitutes. I told them I didn't need anything, I wasn't addicted.

I recall how I got involved with drugs. I was raking one day and this guy had a handkerchief. He used to take cocaine and put it in a handkerchief. He'd snort. I asked him what he was doing. He was a boxer too, from Philadelphia. He told me what he was doing and asked me if I wanted to try it and I said yes. So that's how I got started.

For two years, I did it. When I got caught, you'd have thought I'd clean up. I did for a while, but I got back into it, just before I came back home. I stopped because a guy in the military police told me, "Kangi, they're going to bust you. You'd better cool out." I was able to stop. I never got hooked. That's why I say, God was really looking out for me. As much drugs as I used, I never got hooked.

I used drugs because I liked the feeling. When I started using the drugs, the girls were a by-product. I didn't mess around with no girls because I was preoccupied with the drugs. The only girls I dealt with were drug addicts. I was like a pet, because I was always neat and clean and the girls wanted me around, when they weren't working. These were working girls, and I would stay there. When they'd go do what they do, they'd come back and they would share their drugs with me and we would talk. I had learned to speak Japanese pretty good and I could keep them company.

They called all of us drug users the Eight Balls, and they shipped a whole plane load of us to another place. That's where it really got raggedy for me. My drug use just went rampant, because all of us were into drugs. They weren't going to discharge us, just put us down there. My career came out pretty good, in spite of that, because I came out a sergeant. I would have probably had a higher rank, had I not got involved with drugs. I was court martialed once, but that was for insubordination. I threatened a guy that I was going to do something to him, and they gave me thirty days in jail for that. In spite of all of that, I came out an Airman First Class or a sergeant. It didn't turn out too bad after all.

I was fortunate not to get hooked. I never stuck a needle in my arm. One time, I was tempted to. This girl name Uki, I used to tie her up. I don't mean tie her up [laugh], I mean tie her arm up, you know when you shoot dope in your arm, you tie your arm up so the vein will come up. I used to do it for her, and she would shoot it in. One night, I said, "Why don't you do me?" She said, "Naw, I'm not going to do that to you, because if you do that, you'll be like that for the rest of your life," and she didn't. I was going to do it. She was a real good friend.

In fact, most of my friends were street people, even then. I always liked street people. I don't know why that is. Maybe it has to do with the way I was brought up. The type of people I was running around with were ostracized in the sense that they were so peculiar. They were poor. It just seems like I've always been that way. I've been accused of always seeking strays.

They called me Clean Sergeant, because I used to stay so clean and neat. A lot of guys were bummy. I made friends, and I treated them like human beings. I was never abusive, even when I was using. A lot of times, when people use drugs they get abusive. I was always under control. Even when I was the world's worst, I always managed to do it with class [laugh]. I never stooped.

When I came back from overseas I went to West Palm Beach, Florida. I stayed there for six months before I got out, and basically there was no problem there. It was segregated, but the base was beautiful. I was on the boxing team there, and you always got special privileges, when you were an athlete. Those were the only two racial incidences I had in all the time I was in the military. I did four years in the military.

I came home from the military and my first job was in the steel mill, where I worked for two years. It was rough on me. I was in good shape, but it was just too hard a job. This guy my mother knew had been a precinct captain got me the job in the mills, but that wasn't a job for me, because I was smart.

I wanted to go into stock control where they had an opening. I'll never forget it, you're talking about racism. I was at Republic Steel, and I put in for the job. They called me to interview me. I called the secretary and made an appointment. The man I saw was in charge of industrial relations. When I got to the office, this white lady asked me, "Who do you want to see." I said, "I have an appointment to see Mr. Bond." She said, "Who are you?" I said, "I have an appointment. My name is Kangi." She looked down and said, "Oh, I'm sorry. You didn't sound like you were black on the telephone." I said, "How do black people sound?" When I saw him, I was really amazed at his candidness.

He told me, "You are very qualified for this position, but we're not prepared to hire any black people." This was in 1955, I think. He said, "We're not prepared to hire anybody black, in this kind of position, but I'll tell you what, if you're bold enough to put in for it and come here for this interview, any problem that you have for your duration here, I will help you. Whatever I can do to help you, I will." I didn't stay much longer, because I suffered some very very strong racism. Guys took my clothes. I was in the lockeroom, I was the only black in there and these guys took my clothes. I came to work one day, they had taken all my clothes out of my locker and threw them out on the railroad tracks. When I'd go into the shower, they wouldn't come in there with me. These were Hoosier hillbillies. After that, they would take wire and bolt it to my locker so I couldn't get in to get my clothes. I got the message.

I wasn't bitter. I've always been a Christian. In spite of the fact, I wasn't what you'd call a good Christian because I did a lot of things contrary to what I know God would want me to do but my Christian upbringing was just in me. I don't believe I've ever hated anybody. I've been very disappointed with people in various aspects of my life. I've been taken advantage of, but I knew better and put myself in a position to be taken advantage of. I have always been able to accept responsibility for what I find myself in. I think that's one of the reasons I have no bitterness. I've thought some things should be done to people. I've expressed some things, but with my upbringing, it goes no farther.

One time, I was at Rev. Cobb's house. He was very rich and the one that gave me the money for my first semester of college, along with the neighborhood people. He asked me, "What do you do? I can't find out anything about you." I took pride in that. I always had a mind that if I did some devilment, I'd cover it up. Some people say, "Hey who cares, I do what I want to do," but not me. I never did.

I covered myself, because I knew it was bad. It wasn't something I was proud of. Why would I want to let people know I was doing these types of things? That's why when I was growing up, many of these mothers wanted me to marry their daughters. I fixed them. One time in church (when I came out of service, I was single for so long, people thought I'd never get married) I told them all the things I had done. They stopped bringing their daughters around me. I said, "I'm not what you think I am."

I met my present wife, Jean, at Park Church. It was funny, because I didn't think I'd ever get married. But Rev. Bryant was on my case too. He said, "You got to get married, man." A lot of single women were in that church and boy, it was crazy. These people were matchmaking; I said, "Leave me alone. I know how to meet women." They were playing Cupid. People were inviting me for dinner and everything.

When I was teaching Sunday School, this one girl said, "Why don't you come by; I'm going to fix dinner." I said to myself, no, no sister you're up to no good and these were church ladies. They wanted husbands. They got the word I was single, and I always dressed nice, even though I didn't have a quarter. I just had good clothes and a big job. They were matchmaking like crazy.

When I met my wife Jean, I was forty-five. She's fifteen years younger than I am, and her parents accepted me right away. When I came to Park Church, I had just gotten saved. That's why I went into the ministry, the Lord really put a call on it. Even from a little boy, people used to tell me that I was going to be a preacher. They did. They told my mother.

I did drugs and taught Sunday School. I always went to church, I didn't care what I did. I'd go to church high, but I went to church. I didn't have the relationship with the Lord then, but I went to church. I liked it. That was my social life. I wasn't playing ball now, and I always liked church. So, I stayed there.

When I married Jean, she helped me a lot. I give a lot of credit to her. She didn't know anything about me. She found out about my drug use later. She knew me a good two years and we talked some. I feel a lot of things are better left untold to your wife, in that sense. Now, I have told her, in terms of the way I feel, the reason I act the way I do, because a lot of times she accuses me of being distant. I'll go out in the back. I like to be by myself alot.

My daughter Kaitlin won't let me get away with it. She'll come and say, "What are you doing back here, dad." She'd jump on my lap or grab me, "Come on." I make an excuse like I don't like the TV shows you guys watch, I don't like all that romantic stuff. When you're in a family, you have to interact and I realize that. So, I've worked hard at that, but sometimes it's very difficult. I tell people all the time, if you live one way a thousand years, change is gradual. That's why it takes understanding. My daughter helped a lot. Children help a lot.

My boys, I don't know, my life was so raggedy. I'm proud of Kangi because of his personality. Kangi and my other son, Robert, are from a previous relationship. They are brothers, but they are so different. Robert is quiet and withdrawn and Kangi is not. He always tells me, "Dad, I'm just like you" and it makes me angry, because I wasn't like that. I wasn't abusive like he is. I didn't do people like that. He misuses people. I never did that. I may have done it, but not deliberately, and if I did, I didn't brag about it. In terms of the wildness, probably I was because of this constant thing with sex, young people always want to be such a man. I did that.

People say I don't look my age and that's amazing, because the way I have lived my life, I'm a miracle. It was just the things I've done to myself, in terms of abuse. That's why the way I've evolved is amazing, believe me. I've often felt that I should have not ever been named a minister, but I know what God does with people. He changes them. He takes people from the guttermost and makes them what he wants to make out of them. I've looked in the Bible and read about many people with lives similar to mine. Sometimes, I wonder, how in the world God could forgive me for all this stuff and use me in the way he has.

I changed, because I got sick of myself. I was living on Drexel. I had a bachelor apartment. One morning I looked in the mirror at myself and I was just sick. I was just disgusted with the way I was living, and that's when I came to God.

Education is very important also. Education is a process that begins at the cradle and goes on until the grave. A lot of people give up on it, because somehow they feel they can't learn. That's ridiculous. Education equips you for life. It makes you able to cope and gives you knowledge. I can get very angry at the social situation, but I understand. I understand the politics that says education is important.

Another thing that frustrates young black men is when they do get the education, the jobs are not there. There is prejudice, and that's a reality. You see article after article where even black guys with master's degrees get less money. Kids read and see this, and say, "What's the use." Until this country takes a good look, it's almost like it's designed to keep us out.

Success to me is honesty, and knowing that you've done your best. You've done the best you can do, and you've given it your all. Then you've succeeded regardless of what the grade is. But you see, society does not teach this.

I heard a minister say, and I've adopted it too, "You can always begin again." I love it, because you can begin again. There's hope. I'll never give up on anybody, because God didn't give up on me.

3

Still on High Ground: Joyce's Story

Joyce is a softspoken woman in her fifties. Her affable personality betrays a life of many hardships. Subject to mental cruelty in a marriage that ended in divorce and faced with rearing two children as a single parent, she started her own business. But her greatest personal struggle lie hidden in the shadows of her youth. A learning disability and the inadvertent abuse by well-meaning parents resulted in overwhelming feelings of inadequacy and low self-esteem. Through maturity and a strong religious faith, she was able to emerge from the shadows of her youth a whole person.

I was born and raised in Sanford, Mississippi, which was a country town. My father was a farmer, and we worked for crop owners. We had to get up at 5 o'clock in the morning (I was only about five years old) and go to the field and work all day. My mother went sometimes, but there were twelve of us in the family, so she stayed home most of the time, to take care of the younger ones. She took in washing for white people, while we were in the field. My oldest sister and I had to share doing the cooking. One would go to the field one day and the other one stayed home and cooked. When it was my turn to stay home and cook, I always switched with my sister. She didn't like going to the field. I never liked going to the field either but I would rather go to the field, because I was an outside person and she wasn't. My mother, of course, would make me do the cooking because she wanted to teach us how to cook. I was taught to cook when I was nine years old.

Sanford, Mississippi, it was a small country town. Whites lived on one end and blacks lived on the other end, but there weren't racial riots. Everybody just knew where they belonged. We would work in the white's fields, and they would give us lunch, come to the house sometimes if you were sick, but blacks and whites didn't socialize together. There was the white church on one end of town and the black church on the other end of town. We were separated but in day-to-day living, we had to come in contact with each other. It was as though the white man would say well, the blacks know their place, no need to worry, and that was the case.

We didn't have very much family activities in the South, but we had fun because we did honest childhood things. We jumped rope, rode bikes and we had a movie that came to town once the month. Our biggest thing was getting together in the evening, after we finished all of our chores. The kids would all get together in the yard, of course, the parents would be sitting on the porch, and we played simple children's games. That part of my childhood was happy.

We stayed in Sanford, Mississippi, until I was about eleven years old when my father left and came to Chicago. We left the South for economic reasons. We picked cotton, but they invented a cotton picking machine which meant they needed less and less labor. My father never really had a farm of his own, but we did raise chickens, hogs, cows. We killed hogs and cows for meat. We also raised cane which we turned into sugar. The only thing we really had to buy during that time was flour and milk. We didn't have milk cows. At the time my father decided to came up here, work was very slow. My uncle, who had preceded him up here, sent for my father. That's why my father left and came up here. My uncle lived in Robbins.

I thought we were coming to Chicago, but when we arrived about six months later, we ended up in Robbins, a town where it felt like I had never left the country. Robbins was just like the country town I had left. It was still an all-black town where you might as well say, the blacks lived on one end and the whites on the hill. Here, we went to school with the white children, in the South we didn't. We had a school in the church. Up here you went to school with the white kids. There were conflicts off and on, but no major problems.

Now that I'm grown, and I have raised my own children, I'm glad we lived in Robbins, because I wouldn't have wanted to raise my children in the city. I didn't realize what crime was. In the South, there was no crime, maybe a few fights here and there, but I always felt safe in the South. When we came up here, there was so much crime in the city, I'm glad my father chose Robbins.

When my father came up here, he lived with my uncle and his family, his wife and their daughter. After about six months, my father found a three-room house up on Claire Blvd. That meant two bedrooms and a kitchen. All of us weren't born down South. There were four children, and later three were born here. So, that meant there were nine of us living in three rooms.

In the South, the winters were very, very mild and that first winter up here, I thought I would freeze to death. It was so cold. Somehow, my mother dressed us when we came up here. She made us clothes. My father always worked for white people, and when he came up here he got a job at a car wash. He worked at the car wash for a number of years and all the white people there knew he had twelve children, and they would always give him clothes to bring home. So, that's how we dressed most of the time. But on holidays and special occasions, mother would buy us new clothes to wear. Then my father got a job at the South Suburban Bus Station. He did bus maintenance work and retired from there when he was sixty-five years old.

I remember during the time he worked at the bus station, every Christmas, the bus station would give all the children toys. The company would throw a big party and all the children would go to this party and everybody would end up with some toys. It was the funniest thing that whenever they asked my father how many children he had, he couldn't remember. He would have to bring the papers home for my mother to fill out, because he couldn't remember all the names of the children. My mother would fill the papers out for him to take back to the company, so they would know how many children to expect at the party.

Before my father got his job at the bus station, we were on welfare for a while. During that time, I never understood what welfare was, because nobody looked down on you or said anything about you being on welfare. It didn't cross my mind.   In the community, we were all treated the same. I considered the people we rented the house from as having money, because they had this big house in the front and two little houses in the back, and their children dressed better than we did, but they never talked down to us. We played with them and there just wasn't any difference at that time. We went to school, but when we got up here, they put everybody from the South back a grade.

In the communities where I grew up, your neighbors and the grown ups also raised you. You were afraid to do anything that wasn't right, because if your neighbors saw you, your mother would know about it. They told your parents, and when you got home from school the message was already there. Parents cooperated with the teachers very good. Parents wouldn't accept, this old teacher doesn't like me, or that teacher didn't pass me because she didn't like me. Parents didn't take that. It was that you were wrong. You must have done something to make that teacher angry and to send this note home. So, you got a whipping.

In the neighborhood, we all got along. There was no fighting; even the children got along. There was an east side and a west side, but as far as a lot of gang wars and things, there was nothing like that. We could go out at night and walk the street in the cool of the evening with no fear. This was from about 1954 to 1957. Even through all the struggles I had, I still think compared to children today, I had a good, happy childhood. It didn't seem so then, but as I look back on it and comparing it to today, I had a happy childhood.

My mother stopped her schooling at the 9th grade, but she was a smart person. She was very smart, and I do believe if she had had the opportunity, she would have really made something of herself. She had that drive, that stamina. My father didn't get out of grammar school, but he could write his name, read and count money. He wasn't a smart man, but he has good motherwit. He won't let nobody run over him. He wasn't a dumb person. He never got out of grammar school but he made it through life. He worked. He was a hard worker. Even though he didn't have an education, he worked. My mother worked in nursing homes, but by her having to raise the children, she had to work nights whenever she worked. I admired my mother and father.

There were times I feel I had a hard time in my childhood, because I was a very slow child. At that time, they didn't have special education for slow children. If you were slow in class you were just slow. I remember when I started first grade down South. We went to school in a church. I was really slow and my mother and them thought it was because I was lazy, but I wasn't. I wasn't lazy. It's just that I couldn't comprehend like other children and my sisters and brothers would make fun of me. They called me dumb, and I would cry a lot because I couldn't learn. I just couldn't. I would try so hard, but I couldn't. I guess I had some of my mother in me. I had the stamina, and I promised myself I was going to be something in life. I was going to do something; I was not going to let that handicap me. Everything I have accomplished in life, I had to struggle to do it because of my learning disability. Even now, I have problems, but I never give up. Once I start to do something, I do it. I will not give up and just let it go. I will do it. I do it because, I guess deep inside of me the name calling hurt me so bad until I was determined I'm going to be something. I'm going to do something.

I remember my father helping me with my homework a couple of times. This one time will stick in my mind forever. He was helping me, because I couldn't read well. I had a hard time remembering, and he was helping me with my homework. I was going over the sentence and there was one word in the sentence I couldn't remember. The word was B U T. I would read up to that word, and I could not remember it. He would whip me and make me walk all through the house saying that word, but, but, but. When I got back, he said "Come on start the sentence over again." Everytime I came to that word, I could not remember it. I think what happened was, instead of teaching me, he put so much fear into me until my mind just wouldn't comprehend it. It just wouldn't stick in my mind, because I was so afraid not to know it until I didn't know it. But all that helped me to be where I am today. It taught me to be persistent, and I can say I admire my family.

I admire my father more now that my mother has passed, because now I see him better. Then, I didn't see him as a strong person. I saw him as a weak person, because he would always send us to mother, as if he had no say so. Since my mother passed, he's so different. I'm just glad God gave me the opportunity to live long enough to see the real father in him.

Ten years after they came up here, my father started to drink a lot. He would drink so much, he and my mother would fight. That caused a lot of fear. That affected all of us children differently. I was always afraid. I would wake up in the middle of the night. If I heard a knock, I would jump straight up in bed, thinking it was my mother and father fighting. They fought so much, I wanted my mother to leave my father, because I felt if she left him, then she would be happy, and she wouldn't have to fight all the time. But let me tell you, my mother wasn't a chicken. She would fight back, like a wildcat. But, I used to pray real hard, "Lord, please let my mother and father love each other, let them be happy," but they never were up until the day she died. He took her death hard, because he realized he could have been a better person. And he told us once, "If you all knew the things I did, you would hate me." We encouraged him. We told him no, we loved him. Now, he helps the grandkids. They all depend on granddaddy.

During the time my father drank, I was very confused at that stage in life. I didn't know whether I loved him. I knew I loved my mother, but I didn't know if I loved him. I know I didn't hate him. I resented him, but I didn't hate him. Still, I couldn't say I really loved him. I resented him for fighting my mother. Now he's sick and quit drinking ALL TOGETHER. He hasn't had a drink in over fifteen years. Of course, his heart acted up on him, and he had to give it up. I never thought he would, but he did. He gave it up completely, and now he's our sole support, not support but he's like a counselor to the family. All of my sisters and brothers go to him, and most of the grandkids go to him. I think the thing that keeps him going now is that he's involved in their lives. He complains, but he's going to still be involved. I think that involvement keeps him active.

My parents taught us values. They taught me to be honest. My mother never liked a liar. She taught us to be honest and to obey. That still has an impact on my life. Before I can tell a lie, I'll tell the truth, and I can't stand anybody that is a habitual liar. You can't trust a liar. I try to be a truthful person, because I do feel that way.

When we were little and able to read, my father would make us come in the room with him. He would get the Bible and sit down. He would make us read scriptures from the Bible. Then he would always tell us what the parable meant. He could always explain the parables in the Bible. That's one thing he really did. He taught the Bible to us, not that we were all that interested, but if he said come in, we went in.

Sometimes when he chastised us, he would make it in a parable to teach us. Those are the values that I remember from my childhood.

My father, that I can remember, whipped me one time, and it was nothing like the way my mother whipped me. He was always in the field. It wasn't like, people say today, "When your father comes home I'm going to tell him and he's going to get you." It wasn't like that. My mother took it right then and there. You got it. There was no waiting until your father came home. She did all the disciplining.

We never went to my father for discipline. We would go to my father, and he would always say go ask your mother. We had to go to mother for everything we wanted. My mother did not spare the rod. I really don't know why he always sent us to mother. Sometimes, I thought he just didn't want to make a decision. He wanted to put it all on her. He wanted her to make all the decisions concerning the children. That can throw you off track with who is really the head of the household. Even though he made the money and bought it home, that's where it ended. Now, I see him as a father. I'm very proud of him, and he does so much.

My mother was a very strict person. When I was young and living down South, I can remember one incident when my cousin from Ohio was visiting us. We were up in the church yard playing. The church yard was about four blocks from the house. These two men, who we knew, came by. They lived in the neighborhood. We knew them, and we knew my mother knew them. They asked us if we wanted to go up in the watermelon patch with them to get a watermelon. So, by us knowing them, we said yes, without going home to ask mother. We went up in the watermelon patch and nothing happened. We got the watermelon, and they brought us home.

Mother was standing at the door with her hands on her hips, when we got out of the car. All she said was, "Come on in here." We went in. My cousin didn't know, but I knew from the tone of her voice, we were in for it. She told my oldest brother to go and get three green switches and platt them together and bring them to her. She started. She didn't explain to us we shouldn't have done that because those men could have raped us. She didn't explain nothing to us. She whipped my cousin, and she whipped my sister. She always saved me for last, because she knew I was going to give her a hard time. I was all over the place, under the bed, all over the bed. She whipped us until blood came out of our backs. We had welts all over us. Then she took some kind of salve and rubbed us down. Then she said, "You knew better to go up in that field with those men?" And we were saying, "Mother, we knew them." She said, "You knew better than to leave that church ground." That's all she would say.

Parents in those days didn't explain. We didn't know anything about rape or that we could have been raped. All we knew, if the men had been strangers, we probably wouldn't have gone with them. All we knew is we knew them and our mother knew them. She never explained no more than, "You knew better than to leave that church yard and go up in that field with those men." That's all she ever said. I got quite a few whippings like that.

The last time my mother was going to whip me, she made me strip naked and made my brother get the switches. There was a friend of my grandfather's out in the yard who heard my mother. He ran all the way to my grandfather's house which was about three city blocks. He ran up the road to my grandfather's house and told him my mother was getting ready to whip me naked. I was about ten years old. I had gotten under the bed, and she was scuffling trying to get to me. I don't know what I had done.

My grandfather burst in the door and snatched the switches from her. He told her, "You act like you hate this girl. If I ever catch you trying to whip this girl naked again, I will beat you myself." My grandfather was my refuge. Everytime my mother whipped me, there was no way she could keep me in the house. I would go out the window, the door or whatever was accessible and run. Unless I was in the field, I wouldn't stop running until I found it. I would find my grandfather, and he'd say "Just a minute." I'd say, "Mother's getting ready to whip me." He'd get him a little switch, tap me on the leg and say, "Now come on," and take me by my hand. I loved my grandfather, oh, how I loved my grandfather. He'd take me by the hand, leave his plough in the field and walk me back home and tell my mother, "I done whipped her, now don't you dare put your hands on her." Today, when I see older men, I remember how my grandfather looked. I was eleven years old when he died. I wish he had lived long enough for me to tell him how much I loved him. I never got that chance. So, that was my mother's way, her strict discipline with the switches. I guess she felt she hadn't whipped you enough, if she didn't see any welts. But I loved her.

If my mother hadn't stayed on my back, she used to tell me, "You're not going to be nothing but a tramp," because I wasn't a good housekeeper when I was growing up. My sister would do exactly what my mother told her to do, but I was sort of a tomboy. She'd tell me, "You're going to be a tramp. You ain't going to do nothing but have a house full of kids." She gave me an inferiority complex.

My cousin Janet and I are the same age. There were only two of them, a girl and a boy. My aunt could afford to buy Janet nice clothes, send her to nice schools and put her in college. My mother would always compare me with Janet, and I felt inferior to everybody. I felt I wasn't as good as other people. One thing changed me. I went to visit my auntie in Ohio, and I was out with my cousin, and I heard one of her friends say, "Janet's cousin is prettier than she is." That one thing started me to thinking that I was not inferior to anybody. But, I still grew up with an inferiority complex. I still have some of it. I have to fight hard. I had to fight hard to overcome a lot of complexes in my life.

In those days, people thought if they downed you it would make you better. That's the only reason I can give for my mother's behavior. They downed you, called you names to make you think you weren't going to be this or that. The reason my mother thought I was going to be a tramp was because I was the prettiest one of her girls and she didn't want me to think I was better than them. What she didn't know was I had an inferiority complex anyway. She had already given it to me. She told me that's why she did it. She didn't want me to feel better than the rest of her children. I told her, "Mother, you gave me an inferiority complex."

She never uplifted me. She never encouraged me. I always walked with my head down, but I knew I looked good. So, I grew up to be a very clean person, a very neat housekeeper, because she taught this to me. Sometimes, it doesn't take hold until you get older, but I will never, ever do my children that way. I praise them for what they do good. I advise them. I never, ever talk them down. I think every parent should know that. I taught myself to be strong.

Naturally, my mother taught us about going out with boys and having babies early in life, but when I was about fourteen years old, if my mother hadn't made me go to a party, I never would have gone. I wasn't the partying type. My oldest sister wanted to go and during that time, if there was more than one child, the parent would send another child with that one to make sure that child didn't do anything wrong. So, she made me go to parties. She made me wear stockings. I wouldn't have worn them. I liked to play with boys, but I never wanted a boy to put his hands on me, but my mother saw it differently. By me looking the way I looked, she just assumed I would be that type of person. I could get out there and play with boys all day and not one touched me. I never wanted them to touch me.

Of course, you know your parents tell you about sex, well, my mother didn't tell me about sex. She didn't even tell me about menstruation. She never told me. When I started my periods, I thought I was sick. I didn't know what was happening to me, and they didn't teach you about it in school. I didn't tell her. She found out and then she told me.

I wasn't the fast type of person my mother thought I was. Of course, when you can't keep your eyes on your children's every move, parents can imagine a lot of things. But I was not a fast person. I kept to myself. It seems like I've been a loner all my life. Even when I was married, I felt alone. I was about fifteen years old, and I started to build a wall around myself.

I just started to build this wall, so I wouldn't be hurt, because of my inferiority complex. Then after I got married, my husband hurt me so bad until I didn't think there was nothing else in the world could be worse than a person hurting another person's feeling deliberately. I could never do that. I'm not that type of person. If I can't do you good, I won't do you any harm. Those values came from my childhood, from my father.

My relationship with my parents was pretty rocky, because I didn't know from day to day whether there was going to be a big fight in the house. I felt unloved. I felt my mother didn't take enough time with me, but of course with twelve children how could she. You have to realize some children are more sensitive than others, and I was that sensitive one. I needed that extra attention, but I didn't get it. Nevertheless, I loved my mother dearly, even all of those whippings she gave me. Today, they call it child abuse, but I never hated her. At the time, I might have said I couldn't stand her because of the whipping, but I never thought of her as being an abusive parent. I did quite a few things deserving of a whipping, I admit. But it never stopped me from loving her.

She was mother and deep down inside of me, I knew her. I knew her. She was my mother, and I knew she was doing what she thought was best for me. So, I always loved her. As we grew up to be grown, I was the one she came to with her problems, the problems with the other children. She came to me. She wanted my advice. She consulted me, and we grew even closer. I always thought my mother would live a long time. I didn't care whether my father died or not, because I felt if he would just leave, my mother would be happy. I would have accepted his death much better than I accepted my mother's death. But now, his death would be just as hard for me, because I learned to love him also.

I felt my inferiority complex really showed up in school. I was sort of a big-busted girl then, and the boys would tease me. I thought that was the most awful thing in the world for them to do. They would tease me, but they wouldn't touch me. I also had a teacher name Miss Lee. I couldn't write very well. I couldn't write plain, and she was having us write something down. She came by my desk, looked at my paper and said, "Who do you think can read that chicken scratch?" It hurt me so bad. It really hurt me that she said that in front of all the children. But she would always tell my mother I was the best student she had, because I was always a polite child and I was quiet. I didn't cause any disturbance, and I was obedient. So, in her eyesight that made me one of her best students. Not that I was one of the smartest students, I was just quiet and I obeyed.

I had one grade school teacher, Mrs. Grant. She took to me. I was a healthy child, and I was about her size. She would bring me all her pretty clothes she didn't want to wear anymore. I was about fifteen years old. She would bring all her pretty clothes and try to get my mother to let me spend the night with her. Mother never did. There was a teacher in the South who was leaving Sanford, Mississippi, to go to New York. She begged my mother to let her take me and educate me. My mother told her no. I sometimes wonder today, if my mother had of said yes if I probably would have had a better education, but then who knows, it may not have even turned out that way. I think we all follow God's plan. Sometimes, it may seem wrong at the time but somehow it all works out.

When I got to be about nineteen, I started to really think about God. When we were children, mother got us dressed every Sunday morning, and we went to Sunday school and stayed for church. That was every Sunday. Every Saturday night, my brother's job was to shine our patent leather shoes. We had to iron our clothes that Saturday evening and lay them all out, so we wouldn't have to Sunday, and we would take a bath that night. Of course, we didn't have indoor plumbing. We had those big tubs and we all took a bath that night and mother would get up and give us breakfast and get us dressed. When the bell rang on the church, we were out the door. So, I was actually raised in church, but I didn't come into the full knowledge of religion until I was about nineteen years old.

What brought me into it was, I got married when I was nineteen. For some reason, I always knew how to pray, and my husband did me so bad, every night I was down on my knees praying, "Lord, please don't let this baby come here looking like him. Please don't let this baby come here looking like him." He treated me so bad, I think from then on, I started to really realize that there was really a God. The day my baby was born, I looked at that baby and said, "She looks just like him, just like him" and then it was as though the spirit came to me and let me know the baby looks like him because he would have said the baby wasn't his, if it didn't look like him. That's when I really started to know the Lord and to understand spiritual things, and since then I've just been going the spiritual way. I'm not saying religious. I am a spiritual person.

My husband was a street runner, any woman, anywhere, and I was already a very sensitive person. It didn't take nothing to make me cry, and he knew this. The worse things he could say to me, it was as though he sat and thought about what can I say to her now to just make her feel bad. He said some of the most awful things to me, and I would just cry and cry. It didn't matter to him. He didn't care for me. I was ashamed to walk down the street because people knew I was married to him. They knew what he was out in the street, and sometimes people would ask me, "You're Warren's wife? I didn't even think Warren was married." He lived that type of life, as if he wasn't a married man. That made me go deeper inside myself. The deeper I went, the less I could feel the hurt, and it got to the point where it just didn't hurt anymore. After you're hurt for so long, you just don't hurt anymore.

It's like you are an outgoing person, you want to be, you want to show your love, you want show the person how much you care, but if that person keeps banging at you with all kinds of profanity, it just feels like there's an inner person in you that wants to come out. But that inner person keeps feeling the hurt, so that inner person just goes deeper and deeper until it doesn't feel the hurt anymore. The inner person in me went so deep inside of me until I lost all feelings. I couldn't show love. I couldn't give love. I didn't know how anymore.

One night after we had gotten a divorce, I got down on my knees. It had gotten to the point where I knew I had to talk to the Lord about my feelings. I just felt I needed something in my life that was not there, which was love. I got on my knees and I started praying. I prayed that prayer for a long time, "Lord, please show me how to give love." I guess in the Lord's sight he captured that love, the love I had so much of and didn't have anyone to give it to. The Spirit said, "Give it to me," and I gave my love to the Lord, and I have been a happy, joyous person. Even though I struggle, I still feel that joy, that happiness and I have a love that like God says, knows no bounds. His love is more than any love man could give you. I'm still looking forward to being married one day, if it is God's will. If it's not God's will, I will be just as happy as I am.

I didn't finish high school, but I went to beauty culture school the next year, when I was supposed to go back into the 11th grade. I stuck with it. I finished it. I graduated from it. I made a business for myself, and I raised my children while I had my business. I worked hard, and I always believed in treating customers with courtesy.

I was divorced and all my customers would come in and say, "Joyce, you look as though you never have a problem in the world." That's because I always wore a smile, no matter what. If I had gotten upset with my children and had to discipline them, when I got to my business door, I had a smile on my face. I was having just as many problems as my customers were, but I wore a smile all the time. That made them feel that I never had any problems.

Later, I went to school to become a EKG technician, because I had promised myself when I went into beauty culture I would only work as a beautician for twenty years, and I had been in it for twenty-five years. I always wanted to work in a hospital. My mother wanted me to be a nurse, but that was out of the question. So, I went to school, Medical Careers in Chicago to become a EKG technician. There, I also had a problem with my comprehension. I knew I would, but I had a very nice teacher, and she kept encouraging me. She said, "You can do it. Just try, come on." She encouraged me up until my last test, which I passed. For some reason, if I set out to do something, I'm going to finish it. After that, I did volunteer work at St. Bernard Hospital in Chicago to increase my EKG technician skills. I did it voluntarily to benefit me. After that, I went to work at the university hospital. I enjoyed it.

On my job at the university hospital, there came a letter to the department stating that someone had to be laid off, so they could hire someone in cardiology. I was the third person from the top. There were three people under me. My supervisor decided she wanted me to be the one to leave. Ordinarily, the last one hired is the first one fired, but the last one hired was her pet. She liked her, not that she didn't like me. I had a lot of respect for Terri up until then. When you are working outside of God's law, you don't always do the right thing. In her eyesight, rather than let the last one go, who she wanted to keep, and there were still two others, she made up excuses that I didn't do my work. I didn't do this, I didn't do that.

She went to the head of the cardiology department and told him. He called me into his office and told me, Terri said I wasn't doing my work. Well, I'm very slow, only in one thing and that was editing, working the computer. I could edit, but it took me longer to edit because I had to think. I'm a second thinker. I think twice and speak once. I've done that ever since I was a child, because if I thought twice and did it once, I felt I would do it right. So, it took me longer to edit.

She used that against me. He told me, "We don't want to get nasty about this, Joyce. Terri said you're not editing." I said, there's another girl, Lois and she doesn't even know how to edit at all. Why is she picking on me? She said Lois has other things to do. Editing, you have to learn how to do everything in the department. I said, "Why is it that Lois is not learning how to do everything in the department, if we all have to know it?" He said, "Terri said Lois does other things."

I don't think it was racial. Terri to me is a black person. She says she is unspecified. Her father is black, her mother is Jewish. To me she was black. So, it wasn't racial. It was just that she picked me, because she felt it would be easier to get rid of me than to get rid of anybody else. I cried a lot during that period, because she had me editing. Normally, you only edit maybe once or twice a week. She was trying to prove a point, and she had me editing every day. I can't really do a good job, when I'm nervous. I knew why she was doing it, and I would pray and I would cry, I would pray and I would cry at home, of course.

Her supervisor called me back into the office and said, "You are too slow editing. Now, we don't want to get nasty about this. We can write you up and write you up until you get fired." So, I prayed about it and I said well, I'll quit, I'll quit. I'll be the one to get laid off, because if I get laid off, I can draw unemployment. I didn't hold that against Terri. I really didn't. Other workers in the office were upset about what Terri was doing, and when I got ready to leave one of the girls gave me a present and in the letter in the card she wrote, "I'm very proud of you, Joyce. You stood up and you left out of here with dignity." It was very emotional for me. I cried and I hugged her. A couple of the other girls gave me presents too.

But you know, I think God knew. I think God had a hand in this, because he knew I was getting very tired of that job. I wasn't getting tired because of the patients. I was getting weary, because I just didn't want to work there anymore. God sometimes takes something away from you, but he also replaces it with something else. We just have to be patient and wait. Every since I lost that job, I have not struggled one day. I have met all my bills. In fact, I paid them on time, when I couldn't pay them on time when I was working. I paid them on time and always had food. I never had one day's struggle, and I know God is looking down upon me. I know he sees my struggle, and I know he understands. I know that even though I haven't got a job now, I've got that strong feeling that I'm going to do something. I know I'm going to work. Even it's something I don't really want to do. But now days, a job is a job. So, I still have that feeling nothing is going to bring me down.

The day I walked out of there, I felt good. When I said good bye to my supervisor Terri, she made a move to hug me, but I just couldn't let her think I appreciated what she did to me. So, I'm not hurting for anything, and I know the Lord will provide.

The greatest obstacle in my life was the fact that I could not comprehend. It took longer for me to understand things than the normal person. When I was nineteen years old, after I got married, I taught myself how to write plainly. I wrote every day. I taught myself how to write so people could read what I wrote. One day, I was on vacation and I wrote my sister a card. When I got home, she said "Joyce, I didn't know your handwriting was so nice." I said, "Yes." She didn't know I had practiced all those years to learn how to write.

I was a self-taught person, because I could not comprehend or learn what the teacher was teaching me, so I taught myself. I was a quiet person. I hardly talked at all, because you know the saying, rather than open your mouth and be dumb, it's easier to close your mouth and be thought of as being dumb. So, I never really talked.

I have confidence in myself now. I have confidence, because the Lord has shown me the positive side of myself. I still have those other feelings, but the positive side overshadows the negative side more so now than it did in my earlier years.

Success to many people means many things. Success to me is being able to stand on your own two feet. Being able to provide for your family. Being able to say to other people I love you, you're doing great, to wish others well. Success to me means I raised two children with the help of the Lord, and I worked all those years. I was a hard worker. I was always punctual on my job. I was a success, because I had the strength to discipline MYSELF to do the things I should do and must do. My success has shown my children, you don't have to take any and everything or say I can't do it. I never let my children say, I can't do it, because I never told myself I can't do it. Even now, I just get up and do it. I define my own self. I remember my son was about seven or eight years old and he said, "Mama, I want to be a businessman like you are a businesslady." To me, that meant success.

Many people today don't overcome hardships because that willpower isn't there. You've got to have willpower. You may have a little willpower, but if you keep building on it and building on it and building on it, you will one day get to where you want to be. Like they say, reach for the moon; even though you fall among stars, you're still on high ground. Some people want to operate at a higher level when their level is midway. So, if they can't get to that higher level, they give up, instead of getting to their level, which is midway, which would be their success.

4

The Truth Shall Set You Free: Steve's Story

Steve is a twenty-six-year-old African-American male of mixed racial ancestry. He is married, lives in the south suburbs and is employed as an academic skills/transition adviser at a local community college. He is a compelling young man who speaks with compassion and fervor about his search for cultural identity, the problems associated with his mixed African-American/Cuban racial ancestry, early childhood poverty and his struggle to have his manhood acknowledged in a society that he perceives systematically and insidiously perpetuates social conditions that deny African-American males this right.

I was brought up in a single-parent household, although my grandmother helped raise me. My grandmother came up North with a number of sisters and brothers, during the migration in the 40s and started the family as I know it today. I was born in Chicago.

I didn't find out about my parentage until probably high school. I was always told, if I was ever asked to tell people, I didn't have a father. Me not knowing the scientific aspects of reproduction, just figured I didn't have a father. So, I would just tell them I didn't have a father. They would say, "Well how come your mother's so dark?", because I'm a lot lighter than my mother. I would say, "I don't know. She ate a lot of ice cream." This is fifth grade, but in high school, I thought my mother and father just didn't see eye to eye on things, after she was pregnant with me. So, she decided to have me on her own. It's not as if he walked out on the family, because I've gotten letters today that showed he wanted to come back, but he wasn't the right person. She thought he wouldn't be a good father, my being born out of wedlock. He was Cuban. My grandmother, my mother, two of her sisters, one of her brothers and I believe two cousins all lived in the projects on 38th and Cottage Grove. So, there were a lot of us in one little box apartment.

I can honestly say, my mom worked. I don't remember what the other members of the household did. My grandmother relied on food stamps and things like that, and even with that, I remember she would always say it wasn't enough. I really don't know how she did it. She kept us all fed, and paid the doctor bills. I had an asthma condition. I really don't know how they did it. I spent the majority of my time with my grandmother, because my mother worked during the day. She worked to try to get us out of the projects, as well as help feed the family. My grandmother took care of everybody, during the day. My grandmother was like a second mother. She did a large part of the childrearing. My mom helped, too. They were always there. My grandmother was a person I could tell anything to. She was always on my side. A lot of times when I had problems at school with teachers, she would be the one who came to school.

A lot of people use corporal punishment to discipline children. They didn't do that. My mother had a philosophy that if I treat you like an adult when you're a child, you'll start to think like one. You'll feel you're respected in the household, and you'll respect others. That's actually what happened.

They always stressed education, even though my grandmother never went to high school. She was too busy raising kids. My mother finished high school early and later on in life went to college. They always wanted something better for me than they had. They stressed treat people as you want to be treated, education and family. Everybody was close.

I really don't remember any male role models, as a child. My mother was my male and female role model, because she was always strong. She was always behind me. She always explained things to me about the need to work hard in whatever you do and achieve in the world. All I needed was my mother and my grandmother. As long as I had love, somebody that could explain things to me and the feeling of closeness, that was all that was necessary to me. At times, I would wonder, how I got here without a father, but once she told me I just didn't have one, I accepted that.

I remember a lot of family visits from extended family. Aunts and uncles were always coming by, or we took the bus to go see them. Basically, I would go to church with my grandmother on Sundays, but that wasn't a good experience for me. I would go there and they would say, "Who's that little white boy." So, I stopped going. My mother wasn't a religious person but the rest of the family was. They are to this day. They're all heavily involved in church. I went to church every Sunday, until I got tired of hearing "who's the little white boy," and I stopped going. I didn't see a reason to go somewhere just to be abused on my day off from school. The only other activity, I remember walking five blocks to the grocery store with my grandmother carrying a cart. There wasn't too much you could do in the projects. You walk outside, you get shot. So, you do everything you have to do early, go to school, get in the house, do your homework and make sure you duck when it gets dark.

My grandmother wasn't the youngest person, but she made it a point to teach me the basic maneuvers of the projects; that meant, when it got dark, you crawl. You don't walk in the apartment. You turn the lights out, and when it's time to go to bed, you crawl to your bedroom, because gun shots were everywhere, every night. When I was living in the projects, I got shot at once during recess, and I saw one family friend get shot. That's what we had to do every night. We had bullets shot through our windows, and people running up and down the hallways. The gangs at the time weren't as organized as they are now, but there was a lot of crime. I remember every night, people were shooting from building to building. You'd hear about rapes and everything else in the hallways. So when it got dark, you came in. You couldn't sit outside and enjoy anything, get in and get out. I was about five years old, no older than six, and that's the type of things that went on there. Roaches were constant, and rats the size of a squirrel running down the street. That's just the way it was there, being very poor.

Life in the projects was very stressful and painful. From age two until age of eight, I was a severe asthmatic. Every other week or every other month, I was having a severe asthma attack. A number of those attacks were brought on because of abuse by local school officials. I was very much so the lightest person in the school and I had a certain teacher who liked to point that out. She had had other members of my family in her class before, and she'd always tell me I was the worst one because I was not as dark as that one, and we don't want any little white boys in the class. She even went so far as to have me jumped at recess by various kids in the class. When I went to her for help, she would tell me to go ask this person. As soon as I walked over and asked him, he would scream, "He's looking over my shoulder at my paper." She, having just sent me over, would say, "I just caught you looking over his shoulder. Go stand in the corner." That was total abuse.

Another thing that occurred that triggered my asthmatic condition was, I remember a white substitute teacher one day closing off my Adam's Apple until I had an asthmatic attack. A guy hit me in line. I hit him back, and she came to me, grabbed my throat and closed it. Later on that night, I had two asthma attacks. I also remember a lunchroom incident where the lunchroom attendant was upset that I didn't eat a piece of fat meat they had given us for lunch. So, she took a fork and stuck it in the fat meat and shoved it down my throat until I couldn't breathe. I had another asthma attack right there. That wasn't a time where I had a close group of friends. I had a few friends, a couple but I really didn't feel like I belonged, because the teacher made it a point to make me feel that way. That's only logical. The teacher sets the tone, and if she stands up in front of the class and tell everybody he's different, stay away from him, they're going to do it. I still had friends but not too many, not too many.

The direct physical abuse that directly corresponded to the asthma attacks caused stress. While in the first grade, it got so bad at school that I would feign illness, and it was to a point, psychologically, that it became a real illness. I ended up going to a psychologists, and they explained that I wasn't sick but I was. It was a sickness I brought on psychologically to stay away from school. So, I missed a lot of school during that time and there were a lot of visits between my mother and grandmother to see teachers.

They would go and talk to the principal and teacher. They would argue with the teacher, but as soon as I got back to school, the teacher would make an announcement, "He brought his mother up here today, so I can't say anything to him." It was things like that. It was a war zone everyday for me. It was like I felt isolated in the classroom. It wasn't unusual for me to be stood in the corner for no reason at all. It was not unusual for me to be singled out to point out the difference between my skin color and their skin color.

At the same time, I have to admit, I was wrestling with that fact myself. I would come home and ask my mother what color I was because the teacher said, so and so. She would say, "You're black." I would say, "OK but how come I don't look it." It was the whole thing of not understanding not having a father and everything else, but she would just say, "You are." I would say I am, but I really didn't know why until later on. I don't think there were any white people living on 38th and Cottage Grove. It was totally black. The only white person I ever saw, other than on a television set, was a policeman or a doctor.

Because of the problems, in about the 3rd grade, my mother ended up taking me out of the elementary school in the projects. She sent me to Child City, which was a private school, where I went with Curtis Mayfield's children and a lot of other well-known people in the city. It was on 82nd and Bennett. I guess it was a school for exceptional children. It was a private school. It was supposed to be a real good school. When they had to move, I went back to my former elementary school.

At five or six, I was under a lot of control. You don't let five- or six-year olds run around, anyway. My mother got enough money together, and the two of us moved from the projects to 47th and Greenwood, which was a nice area. She got married while we were there. I never considered him a stepdad. I always considered him my mother's husband or my sister's father. They had the baby, I believe, there. He was a truck driver. It was him, my mom, me, my sister and my dog.

I just never felt a closeness to my stepdad. He made a point to treat his daughter better than he treated me. I guess like with most fathers, he competed with me. He would always say, I used to do this at your age or I used to do that. He also brought into the household the practice of calling me names, which my mother later picked up. She had never done that before, but I guess after being with him for so long, it was always you're stupid, you're dumb, you ask stupid questions. That could have easily turned me into really feeling I was stupid, but there was something inside me. Whether it was me calling my grandmother and her reinforcing my inner strength or whatever it was, I just resolved I'll show you how stupid I am. I'll make it. I'll make it and you'll regret saying it. That's basically what happened.

There's not one incident of the verbal abuse, because it was a daily thing. The nurturing was gone. My mother was trying to figure out, since she had one child by him and one that wasn't his, how to place him into the family to make him feel at ease. Eventually, they got a divorce. It was very violent, including physical abuse. To this day, I hate his guts. At the very beginning of their marriage, I told my grandmother I predicted a divorce within the next five years and I was right.

We moved to Harvey. It was a big change. It was perfect timing. Harvey was perfect at the time. It was a nice mixed area, I would say probably still majority black, but it was so nice and clean. There were things to do, Little League and other things. It wasn't a question of what illegal things can I get into. I was feeling, this is what life is suppose to be like, good schools and everything else.

Living in Harvey, pretty much everybody had a good attitude toward children. They didn't treat you like a lesser being, like hello, how are you, that type of thing. I made friends very quickly and everybody was neighborly. It wasn't unusual to see people going door to door visiting and things like that. It was a really nice neighborhood. The people were very close. Everybody had pride in their property, and everybody worked as far as I remember. Drug dealing wasn't a problem, at that time. In fact, drugs and gangs as I remember didn't come until 1980 and I was there, I believe, starting in '75 or '76. I was eight years old.

I don't think the teachers in Harvey were insensitive, it was just a matter of me trying to catch up, because I had no math skills whatsoever and that's hurt me to this day. That was probably my main problem. A lot of problems, basic English structure and things like that, I was always a well-spoken person, because my mom spoke to me as an adult and she's a very excellent speaker. It was just the technical aspects of education. The only thing I can say I was actually advanced in was history, because that was my first book. I started studying history maybe from the age of four up.

It was my deceased aunt's history book from high school, and while she was still there, I remember I used to read it every day, and I got this fascination. I would look through it and see the maps. I told them to buy me little plastic soldiers, so I could re-create battles. My grandmother gave the book to me, after she died. She said, "You want it. You read it all the time. Take it." I would read it every day, until I memorized it.

Probably, the teacher who stands out the most in elementary school was a history teacher, Roosevelt Keys. I don't know if you want to call him a role model, but I remember he showed a little more closeness and a little more respect for me than the rest of the teachers. There was more of a connection there. He took my interest in history even further. It was more than a matter of, I'm telling you, I'm giving you this subject on the blackboard, copy it, do the homework and that's that. If I wanted to sit after class and discuss things with him, it wasn't like child/student. It was like two intellectuals speaking. I respected him for that. He also got along very well with all the other students. He was just a likeable person. Two history instructors in college also had a positive impact on me, and there was a teacher in high school, Ogden Miller. I liked anything that had to do with history. So, of course, those teachers stand out in my mind. They were the ones who gave me due respect, that I could exchange dialogue with, who treated me, I don't want to say equal, but gave me my due respect.

Harvey began to change, in my estimation, in 1980. I graduated from eighth grade in 1980 and started high school. As soon as I stepped into high school, the school was changing. It wasn't so bad during the first two or three years, but the last year, I almost lost my life on a number of occasions. It got so bad my last year that even if you weren't in a gang, you still were a target. Before that, you'd hear about the Disciples fought the Vice Lords, but after that you started to hear about or see people getting beaten in the streets because they weren't in a gang. It was like, if you are we're going to get you and if you're not you're still a target because you're not. I saw a number of beatings. I was shot at a number of times, and had knives pulled on me, when I was in high school.

Once the composition of the school changed and became more of a gang atmosphere (gangs and drugs), the people I grew up with in Harvey who were all close, broke up for some reason. Half of them ended up in one gang, half ended up in another. They forgot all about the ties they had formed over the years. It was a matter of, he's a Vice Lord, we can't talk to him or he's now a Disciple. As for me, I never joined either one of them. Growing up with these people, I had friends on both sides. Thinking logically, that was the best thing to do anyway. Joining either one of them would have made me a target. This way, at least, I could shield myself by having friends on both sides. It wasn't a fabricated thing, because they were my friends. I just made it a point to get along.

In my senior year, I ended up having to go closer to one side than the other. I was with a friend one night going to a baseball practice. He got robbed by a member of one gang. They didn't rob me. Other things like that happened, just say going down the street. It was a matter of looking at who was giving me the most flak.

I had a mob waiting for me after a basketball game one night. It was the same gang I drifted away from. I was dealing with a young lady. I got tired of how she was acting. She was a very abusive person, and I got tired of trying to wait for the good to come out in her. I told her I was through with her. She got mad and went and got a gangbanger boyfriend, told him I was hanging up in her tree naked, screaming out her name and making death threats to her house. When you're talking to a gang member who has no interest in education or intellect, it doesn't make a difference if any of it makes sense or not. So, he made sure people followed me to class. I had people following me and my friends after school. There was this group of at least sixty people waiting for me after the game. I had a friend with me. They came up to him and said, "Move away from him. We're about to move on him." As it turned out, my friend had a brother who was in this same gang, and he told them you're not touching him. I got away. They ended up jumping one of my friends later on, because he was my friend. It was all over this girl.

It was very complicated, and from then on I couldn't deal with my friends in this gang, because the gangs were more important than our friendship. I started leaning more towards my friends in the other gang. Therefore, I was identified as a member of this gang. Up to a point, I really didn't care. I was actually ready to join that gang, but I thought about it and I knew I wanted my education beyond any of it. I knew I was going away to school. I figured this is senior year, I can last for another six months and get out and go on with my life.

I didn't have a social life because the color stigma still followed me, even though I didn't have teachers pointing things out. In fact, I was a lot more accepted. In Harvey, when they would come into the room to take census and say, all the black people stand up, I was stigmatized and didn't know whether I should stand up or not. I would have people in the class in 5th and 6th grade say "Get up here. You're one of us." It felt good. I was accepted for once.

The girls were a different story. One thing stands out in my mind. It was 4th or 5th grade. They used to play a game called "Catch a Girl, Kiss a Girl." They kicked me out of the game when the girl I was chasing turned around and said, "Get your white ass away from me." So, I never had a social life in grade school. I felt stigmatized, isolated and ostracized. I never went to parties or learned how to dance. To this day, I don't dance, and I don't go to parties. That basically cut me out of social life in high school, as well.

I felt more accepted with the friends I had grown up with all this time and went to the same high school with. We formed very close friendships. It was just that I didn't have any life with females. My first three years, there wasn't even a chance of me getting close to anybody. Nobody was interested. It was just a matter, that's Steve. He's a nice guy, but that's it. Consequently, I never even felt women would be attracted to me. In fact, I thought I would go through life being a virgin, to be honest with you. I even went through a phase where I started calling myself Lancelot. I read *Once and Future King.* He was a virginal knight. So, I just figured that would be me. My friends were encountering girls, freshman, sophomore, junior year. I never had a story to tell. They would say, "I got a girl calling me, I got to go home." That never happened with me, at least until senior year.

Senior year, my friends and I were tired of being just the nice or goofy guys, because we were always making jokes. We wanted to make a statement our last year out. At the time, the big thing was break dancing. We formed our own break-dancing club, one of the first break groups in the school. We had the best-looking outfits and everything. So, we drew attention to ourselves. It was a thing, I guess you see it with sororities and fraternities in the college, the person is not attractive until he joins a group. The colors make him attractive. After that, we had people flocking to us, "Oh what's your name." By that time, I had lost all inhibitions, because I told myself, "I've gone sixteen years without a girlfriend, without any contact with females of an intimate nature. I'm not going to worry about it anymore. I got one year left. I'll go ahead and go for broke. If I get rejected, if I don't get rejected, fine."

I went headlong into it with no thought of being rejected. It was just a matter of, this is my last year, let's go for broke. It doesn't matter. That in addition to the fact that we had become this new great break club, even though we didn't break at all, it was just a matter of the colors.

When I started to break out of my shell, feeling that maybe I wasn't so bad, or all the people who through life told me I was too light or too ugly, or too this or too that, maybe they were wrong. So, high school was pretty fun. Senior year was equally good and bad. Bad because I was shot at a number of times, even to the point where a group of boys drove on the high school lawn. We were going to a party one night, and they jumped out with machetes. It just so turned out, we knew them. If we hadn't known them, we would have fought right there and someone may have died.

Sports played only a very small role for me at Thornton High School. We always had these near-professional players at Thornton.

We always had a good team. So, there was no way for me to make the team. I always tried out for baseball. I was always a baseball player. Harvey was an ideal community when I first moved there. I got involved in Little League and was pretty much involved in Little League up until high school. Little League was over, I believe, at twelve. I tried out for the high school baseball team a couple of times, once I reached high school, but I never made it. The coach always had a way of, even though the community and the high school was maybe 80–85 percent black, not choosing blacks for the team. Perhaps that stereotype, subconsciously, seeped in that black people weren't as good at baseball as white people. So, he would always take the people from Dolton or Riverdale, even though the majority of the population to choose from was black. The team somehow always ended up whitewashed with maybe one or two blacks.

What was funny is when it came to Summer Leagues. We had a Babe Ruth League in Harvey, but it was sporadic. One year it would go and the next it wouldn't. You could play up to the age of fifteen. A number of the players, who got cut from his team, ended up playing better than those that made his team. They were getting accolades and starting while his players sat on the bench during Summer League. It was kind of funny. After age fifteen, there was a lack of sports activity in Harvey itself. I would say that contributed to gang activity. There were no activities. The only thing you could get into, if you didn't have a good home life and given the environment and the declining economic climate of Harvey, was gangs and the drugs. If you didn't have any type of activity after school, you either stayed in after school or come outside and be a target. If you didn't want to be a target, you joined one of the gangs. That was your only alternative. There was no escape.

You couldn't go into any of the neighboring communities to do anything, because if they didn't tell you you had to be a member of the community to join their activity, they would just tell you straight out like they told me, "We don't want any niggers from that city." So, you were stuck in your own community. What is there to do? I could stay in the house and be a clam, or I could go outside and try and live. That meant being in with the social flow at that time, which were the gangs.

Then there was your basic racism, taking away your cultural identity or teaching you that you're nothing or meeting your people with violence so that the only thing they can do to relieve themselves is to create violence upon themselves. In Harvey, there wasn't much to do with the Park District or anything else. So, you looked at a neighboring community, like when I looked at Riverdale Basketball Leagues. Some of the white guys at my high school were from Dolton or Riverdale. They would say, "Why don't you come play with us?" They gave me the number of somebody that was over the program. I was supposed to call them. I called and he said, "Where do you live?" I said, "I'm from Harvey." Maybe my vocal style wasn't as polished at the time, but I don't care. The fact is, when he heard I was from Harvey, whether it was my tone of voice, the way I spoke or the fact that I was just from Harvey (by that time it was about 85-90% black), he said, "We don't need niggers from Harvey." Yes he did, over the phone. I had a friend sitting with me. We were all set and the guy said what he did.

Many times you look at television and see these stories about the Bronx, young Italian men or young Irish men, having nothing to do, no type of community activities, hang out on the street corner, set fire in the garbage can and sing. That's a romantic idea. The only thing we could do in Harvey was that. At the time, the big type of music was hot mix, where the DJ scratched things up on the radio. So, we would all get out on the corner rather than be involved in a gang.

We would sit out there and whoever could sing would try to croon. It wasn't unusual, whether it was at the street corner, by the mailbox or in front of one of our houses, for a white policeman to come by and say "Get away from here." We'd say, "But this is in front of my own house." The police would say, "So what, I said get away from here." We'd tell them, "You say I've got to get away from in front of my own house?" They'd say, "Yeah, go in the house. Get away from here." We'd say, "What are we doing?" "All we're doing is singing." They'd respond, "I don't care. I'm going to charge you with drugs in a minute." We'd tell them, "But we don't have any drugs." They' say, "So what, I'll charge you with it anyway." That wasn't unusual.

Many of these policemen don't come from your community. Therefore they have no reason to wish to see your community do better. They have no reason to care about the community. Therefore, they come to your community, and consciously or subconsciously act on stereotypes, thinking these are a bunch of animals anyway, I'll treat them this way or that way. They stir up gang violence and everything else.

When I was in high school, it was not unusual for a policeman to go to a party and see both gangs there. They would let one of the gangs go to give the impression that they were the favored gang. The other gang would get lined up against the wall, and they would each get hit in the crotch (to be nice about it) with the nightstick. That way, since they couldn't direct their anger at the policeman who was the man, the man with the badge who had the seal of approval from white America, they directed their anger at the other gang. They're the favorites of the police. They made this happen to us. So, when the police weren't around you end up shooting and fighting each other. The police were good for that. That's what they did.

I didn't have any black history to speak of until college. That also compounded the problem. Trying to feel you are a member of something and then on top of that, you don't know what that something is, because nobody had a cultural identity. This is the problem even today in schools. That ended up coming to a head, my first year at Southern Illinois University. That's where even though I had always known I was black, I began to feel black, I guess you could say because I actually got an idea as to what my culture was. I actually had my first black history course.

Southern Illinois University was a very racist campus. We had very few black students and they stuck together. Even though all the way up until this time my mother had always told me about racism (she was a marcher in the 60s), I guess I had been brainwashed by the thought of the perfect America. I never questioned why the north section of Harvey was all black and poor or why certain things were this way or that way, until I got to Southern Illinois University.

I got to see racism firsthand. Before, there was the matter of blacks not feeling that I was a member of the group. Now, I'm part of the group because whites see us all the same. There were a lot of racist things, hearing "nigger" not on TV or when someone passes you on the street and screams out a car, but actually seeing groups of racists with a face. It was no longer a faceless enemy.

There was a lot of closeness there. The brothers there just bonded together. I guess that's what happens on campuses when you're a minority. When you go to a black campus, you usually don't see any black student groups. You see groups, but nobody feels a need to be close. However, when your back is against the wall, you join together. We had people that just gravitated together whether they were from the west side of Chicago or the north side, from the south suburbs or the north suburbs, whether they were a Vice Lord or a Disciple. Gang affiliation went out the window, when I went to college. It was just a matter of we are black. I actually started to understand exactly what racism was. Why there was a need to have black unity.

When it was lunch time, we all left the room at the same time, from all these different dorms. We all met together in the middle of campus, simple strength, twenty-five black men in an area of white people and they moving out your way, walking into a cafeteria, pulling five or six tables together, sitting down all at once and holding hands, that type of thing.

That's how it was. If anybody came back and said, this person said something to me. This person made a racist statement to me, or this person did this, it wasn't one person or two or three, it was the group that was now at their door. We didn't have to feel like a minority. We were self-contained. We take care of ourselves and don't mess with any of ours, because we'll mess with you. It was just that simple. It was also intra-group nurturing, studying, going out together. There was never one of us alone. It was very easy, because you would always hear the word "nigger" down there.

I could see things, because I was getting this awareness now. I would see a black person who hung out with a group of five, six white people, and think they were part of the group. They would be laughing, sitting with them and when they weren't around you would hear, "that super nigger" or something like that and this person was right back laughing with them the next day. You could even see that happening to the person's face, but because they had no cultural identity, they would accept it and take it. "So what he called me a nigger, what does that mean? Am I really black, not really." The experience of being in that group, which we called SIU Circle, was a big part of my life. Some of us stay in contact to this day and some of us don't. But we will all be bonded forever.

The greatest obstacles I've had to overcome were poverty, the color problem and the search for cultural identity. Cultural identity for the simple fact it was never taught. I think all of those are interconnected. If you aren't taught your cultural identity, taught that you have something to be proud of, you may start to feel more at ease in poverty. If you don't know how you got in the situation of poverty, it's very easy for you to start placing blame.

Many times, that's what happens between blacks of different shades of color. We'll say, they get it better than us or this group gets it better than us. The same thing happened between the blacks and the Irish. It boils down to poverty. You always place blame, because you feel somebody is taking what you have, and the fact is none of you have very much of anything, and the only person that's laughing is the person that has. All of this is interconnected and the main problem, which in essence is racism.

I always knew the value of education. I always knew I wanted to be educated. I was already educated. Before I knew it, I was reading books when other people were playing with toy guns. I was really reading. My mother always told me, you have to get an education in order to make it in this world, and you're going to meet racism head-on. At the time, I was very young. I didn't understand that, but in college I did. You're going to meet racism head-on, and you've got to be able to meet it on equal terms. If you have your piece of paper from college, they won't be able to stop you from coming in through the door, and if they do, you'll have recourse. You'll know what to do. I prefer to make a separate door. I don't want to come in through anybody's door. I want to make another door where I won't have to ask somebody to let me in, making them reject me. I'll be the one letting people in, my people. It's very simple.

The fact is, some people fold under the pressure of poverty. Some people never make it out of the ghetto. If all you see every day is oppressive conditions, and you don't have any hope, and not knowing or having a sense of culture or knowledge of self, you begin to accept those things.

Then there is the electronic media. I go outside my door, I see drug dealers and gangbangers. I don't know why they are there. I can only repeat what I hear white people say on TV. They're black inner-city youth. I go back and watch my TV, and all I see on TV when it comes to a crime is, this black man committed this crime or this black this or this black that. Then, I turn on National Geographic. All I see are Africans jumping around in grass skirts. Not being taught anything about my culture, not seeing it as beautiful, you see this as primitive. The fact is, who's qualified to call something primitive. If you had a knowledge of your culture, you would see that as beautiful. Without being taught anything from a cultural perspective or the cultural perspective of Africa and not having any black teachers to instill it in you, you can't appreciate your own culture.

You can have a white teacher teach black history, but if they never lived the experience or don't really have an interest in instilling that feeling of blackness in you, it's not going to do anything. The fact is, you still have to be taught it. If you're not taught it, and you don't have a role model to show it to you and you're bombarded every day with the negative images on television or your environment, without being able to understand why it is like that and think about how you might be able to change it, many times you become a victim. It's that simple. The reason blacks are not proud is not illogical.

Take the Los Angeles Rodney King ruling, for example. If you feel powerless, many times you snap, because you can't attack those bringing that feeling of powerlessness or bringing this oppression upon you. So, you lash out at the person who's closest. The person who's closest who may not be able to retaliate against you. I'm saying if a black person commits a crime against a black person, they have a lot less to fear, generally, than if they committed it against a white person. That's a simple fact. For example, my boss fires me today and hires a white guy in my spot and I'm more qualified. I come home and whether I'm a woman or a man, I strike out at my kids or my spouse. I just struck out at somebody in my household who is available. I don't have to go fifty miles away to attack my boss and I won't get arrested for attacking my wife or kids. It's an immediate response, and you feel you can get away with it. It's logical. To paraphrase Stokely Carmichael, when a people are oppressed, they will eventually take on the characteristics of their oppressor to free themselves. To take that a little bit further, those characteristics will eventually be turned against themselves.

I've written one book fully, and I contributed to another. My book is called *Words From An Unchained Mind*. I chose that title, because I felt I had some things to say. Many people who may feel the same things as me, may not feel anybody wants to listen. I knew I had something to say, and I wanted to say it. I'm not going to admit that somebody's more qualified to say something than me. I've lived the same experience or even a more deathly experience than many people. So, how can a person who's wearing a suit and a tie sit and watch and comment on the problems of the inner city or inner city black youth when they haven't been in the inner city, and I came up from that. It's never going to leave me. I had many things to say from the perspective of a black male, dealing with many different issues.

I believe it was Jean-Paul Sartre who said (and this is a paraphrase), if you only define success as achieving goals, you set yourself up to fail. My definition of success is that you have given your best effort possible. If I tried to win the race and I didn't win, but I gave it my best effort, I succeeded, because I did the best I could.

5

A Place to Call Home: Juanita's Story

Juanita is a soft-spoken woman in her forties. In speaking with her, one is struck by her sensitivity and kindness. She is a woman who has used her personal life experiences as the motivating force in making a difference in the lives of others. Reared most of her life in a foster home, her life story is one of a search for love and a sense of belonging.

My mother and father were never married. I was their only child, although they had children by other people. The unique thing about me is I have two sets of parents, because at age four, I was put into the foster care system in the State of Illinois. I lived with that family from age four to about age eighteen or nineteen. I don't really know a whole lot about my biological parents. I found out some things, after I became an adult.

My foster parents had seven children of their own. It was a middle-class family. My foster mother stayed home to take care of the children and my foster father worked for a power company. It appeared that he was very successful in his job. I don't remember what he did, but we were a middle-class family. Their youngest daughter is ten years younger than me. Most of their children were pretty grown up when I came to live with them. One of my siblings, my brother under me, was placed in the foster home with me. A middle brother was placed in another foster home. My biological mother had three other children. She had six children in all, but the last three she raised herself.

I remember on a lot of occasions growing up, my foster parents considered my brother and me their contribution to society. They often put us on display, saying we were their foster children and our mother abandoned us, and they were doing their best to raise us and help us overcome the fact that we came from a bad seed. I remember hearing those words often, and I think my self-esteem suffered as a result of that.

Their children often looked down on us. We weren't ever really considered part of the family. We were considered the foster children and were sort of set apart from their own children. In some ways growing up, my foster family treated us like slave labor or hired help. I shouldn't say hired help, because we didn't get paid for it. We had to do all the chores around the house. We even painted and cut the grass. We did everything. In fact, we didn't have a lot of time to go outside and play like other children. Some of the kids in the neighborhood would tease us, because we were always working. They would say things like, "You never get to go anywhere. Every time we look around you're working. You never go anywhere." We weren't invited to parties, because they knew that we couldn't come, so they didn't invite us.

My foster parents believed that no kid should be idle, except their kids didn't work as hard as we did. They had chores, but my brother and I basically took care of the home, repairs, painting, anything that had to be done. The home we lived in on Eggleston had ten or twelve rooms. It was pretty big. My brother and I had our own bedrooms. When we moved on Peoria, the house was smaller, but they built an addition which allowed us to have our own space.

The values my foster parents taught me was that we had to rise above the fact that we came from a bad seed (my mother was considered a whore) and that we were going to be no good when we grew up, if we didn't try to overcome it. They did instill in us that education was very important and that it was important that we complete our education. We were taken to church a lot, and I had gotten to the point where I didn't like church very much, because I didn't quite understand what was going on there, plus the kids there made fun of us. So, most of my childhood was spent cleaning, cooking, taking care of the house. They even taught me to manage the money of the household. I learned how to pay the bills. I was in charge of all of that. My brother was pretty much into taking care of the house and painting.

My foster parents believed in corporal punishment, and we received quite a bit of that for anything considered wrong. Discipline was very severe at times. We rarely got hugged or complimented for anything we did, and if we did anything they considered wrong or bad, we would get these terrible whippings. I remember in high school, I had so many welts on my body, I used to cut P.E. because I was embarrassed for people to see how severely I was beaten.

My relationship with my foster parents was never what you would call a loving relationship. In fact, I think it was based more on fear. It was more fear of my foster mother than of my foster father. My foster mother administered most of the punishment, most of the whippings. In fact, all of the whippings, because I can't remember a time when my foster dad hit me. He would sometimes come to our rescue. Like I said, it was a fear kind of a relationship. I wasn't very loving, even though maybe she did love us in her own way which I had come to terms with as an adult, but as a child, I can't ever remember feeling very loved. There was always a fear of being sent back to the foster care system and being put into another home. That as a threat they always held over us. "If you don't behave, if you don't do this correctly, we always have the option of sending you back." That caused great fear, because we didn't want to have to repeat over again being put into another home. Even though things weren't always the best there, we felt that was the best place for us at that time.

Family activities included going to church, maybe going on a Sunday drive sometimes. Basically, we stayed home and did chores. We worked a lot around the house. We barely got a chance to go to the movies, and TV was very much restricted. We did not look at a lot of television, even though we were the first people on the block to have a color TV. We were very restricted in terms of looking at it. I became a bookworm. I read a lot. It was a way of escaping, and I stayed in my room a lot. We didn't do a whole lot of things as far as playing games or anything together that much. Going to church was the big thing in our family.

I went to elementary school, finished up eighth grade and then attended Harlan High School. I liked school. It was an escape from home. It was a place to go when I wasn't at home. I loved to read, and I excelled in school. In fact, I was an A/B student pretty much all the time I was in school. My brother, on the other hand, rebelled a lot and got into trouble. He got suspended for fighting. I guess it was his way of letting off steam. I was more like an introvert. I kept things inside of me, and I didn't voice my opinion much on anything. I was sort of like a wallflower. I was quiet in the classroom. The teachers didn't have to worry about me talking much. I was just an introvert, into my self, quiet.

I thought I got a good education for that time. The Chicago public school system was a pretty good school system I would say, unlike it is today. It was more stable. Neighborhoods were stable; kids didn't move around a lot.

My teachers were teachers. I can't remember any single teacher that stands out in my mind. I was a quiet kid in the classroom. I did what I was supposed to do. I earned good grades and I never really had any special relationship with any teachers. I was never singled out by any teacher to feel special, but I respected teachers a lot. I decided when I was very young I wanted to be a teacher. I guess I saw teachers as having power. They were pretty much their own boss, which I felt I wanted when I grew up. They had an effect on society, and I wanted to be able to contribute to that. So, I guess that's how I perceived my teachers, even though I didn't really have any special relationship with them.

I feel the greatest obstacle I had to overcome in my life is that I never really felt I fitted anywhere. Even though I had two families, a foster family and my biological family, I didn't really fit in with either one. With my foster family I was an outcast, and with my biological family, I never really knew them, so they were just like invisible people. I felt if I could fit in somewhere, I could find myself. I could find out more about myself. I could be someone.

When I was nineteen, I moved out of my foster parents home. I remember the very day it happened. I wanted to attend a party, so I asked for permission. I finally got permission, but I had to be home at 10:00 P.M. I was eighteen, almost nineteen years old. So, I went to this party and at 10:00 P.M. (everybody knows a party isn't even starting at 10:00 P.M.) I didn't leave. I stayed later and later and eventually, I had stayed all night. When I came home the next day, my foster mother had a tree limb she had broken off one of the trees in the backyard, and she proceeded to beat me with it. She beat me and she beat me, until she almost broke my arm. I said, "This is it. I'm out, I'm out of here." My foster parents said, "If you move, if you go, then you're not coming back, and you can't take anything that we've ever bought for you."

So, I left with the clothes on my back and I moved in with a girlfriend and her family. After living there for maybe a couple of weeks, I decided, this is worse than being at home. I got a job. I started working at the Post Office, and I eventually had enough money to move into my own apartment with a roommate. That's how I got to be on my own.

I had started dating, which I had never done in high school or ever, actually. I wasn't sexually active, because I had the religious upbringing that stated sex was dirty and I didn't really want any part of it. So, I wasn't sexually active until I was almost twenty-one. I was dating and eventually met this guy. I became serious with him, and we got married. I think I married him because I was still looking for this family atmosphere, wanting to belong. That's the wrong reason to get married. In fact, I know it is. The marriage didn't work out, and he was doing drugs. I'd never been exposed to drugs before. I didn't even know what they were. I had never seen anybody on drugs. I decided this isn't for me, and after a while of the abuse and the people he'd bring home on drugs, we broke up.

By that time, I had a baby. He was about two years old. I finally decided I needed to go back to school, because I was tired of working these little penny-ante jobs making no money. I felt I had more potential than that, even though I didn't quite know what my potential was. In fact, I didn't know at all what it was.

Having no money, having a baby, I was able to get on public aid and qualify for some state grants. I started going to Kennedy-King College, all the time still dealing with an asshole for a husband. Excuse me, but that's what he was. I continued to go to school at night. I still excelled in school. I was an "A" student, so I was able to win a scholarship. I took this scholarship and applied to Roosevelt University where I continued to pursue a bachelor's degree. In the meantime, I'm a single parent raising a child, going to school fulltime and working parttime and on public aid. It was quite a struggle.

My foster family wouldn't have anything to do with me, and I didn't know anyone in my biological family, so I was pretty much out there on my own. My brother had moved out by this time, but he stayed in my foster parents' home a little longer than I did.

Going to Roosevelt University, I'm meeting a lot of new people. I'm meeting people who I thought were pretty much on the ball, black women who were smart and aggressive. I'm starting to hang out with these people, and I'm starting to get some confidence within myself. I'm starting to go to meetings and join social clubs. I'm growing up. I'm having my own ideas about things, but I still had this void. I was thinking, I never really had a family and I never will, so you've still got to go out there and make it. You can be somebody. You don't always need a family to do that.

It took me quite a while to reach that point. In fact, my brother and I used to have a lot of talks together, and we came to realize that if we had been brought up by my mother, we probably would not have had any of the tools our foster parents gave us. Even though they were abusive at times, they did give us tools to become independent people so that we could take care of ourselves. So, I graduated from Roosevelt University, and I got my first teaching job. I taught special education for three year. All the time, I'm feeling more confident about myself. I feel like I'm closer to being somebody than ever before.

I always thought I wanted to leave Chicago. I always felt Chicago was a hindrance to me, and that I had done everything here I possibly could do, and I wasn't going to grow any more unless I left. I had this friend who lived in Ontario, and he used to call me up and say, "Come on up. You've got your degree. You can probably get a job here." So, in 1985, I checked out Ontario. I thought it was rather different, and I didn't know how I was going to fit in, but I knew I had to take the chance, because I had to get out of Chicago. Plus, I had a twelve-year-old son, and I wanted him to be out of Chicago too.

So, we moved to Ontario in 1986, with the help of my friend, and I got a job there. In fact, I had three half-time jobs before I was hired by the school district as a teacher. I was a substitute for the school district for a year.

In the meantime, my friend was helping me, and I moved into his house. I realized here's a man who really cares about me, who really has my best interest in mind. I needed to take a look at that. We eventually got married, and I've been working as a teacher for the school district.

I've come to the conclusion that I am somebody. I'm smart. I'm aggressive. I like to go after things I like to do and do them right. I feel I have leadership abilities, and one day maybe I'll pursue being a principal. I don't know. It depends on a lot of things.

All through these years, I had a best friend; her name was Debra. She passed this year which was a great loss. We helped pull each other up by our bootstraps. We'd give each other pep talks all the time. I encouraged her, and she encouraged me. I met a whole lot of black women who were role models for me.

I met my dad when I was twenty-five years old, and that part of my life where I wanted to know my father was finally filled. The disappointing part about it was he was sick and old and tired and didn't have any money. I was disappointed, but I said, "Can't let that stop me." I should be grateful for just knowing my father. I developed a relationship with him, but my mother and I right now are not speaking, for various reasons. I've come to the conclusion my mother doesn't care for me very much. I guess one of the reasons is, because she didn't raise me and she doesn't have that motherly love, which is OK.

I'm very grateful that my mother didn't raise me, because I don't believe I would be as far in life as I am today. I am close to other people in my family. I still converse with my brother in, Chicago. He has two little girls. One of them he named after me. We're very close. I'm close to my mother's sister, my aunt, and we converse. I have cousins. So, I do have members of my family I've become close to which kind of fills the void I've had all my life.

I just had to come to the conclusion that no matter where you start from, you can always make it better, if you want. You can sit there and cry the blues and blame things on other people. You can say nobody loves me and I can't, but after a while, that gets to be very tired. You have got to wake up and see that you can do for yourself, no matter what your background. I believe I got that from my foster family. Even though at the time I didn't realize it was there, it came through for me much later in life.

I became a Christian, and I feel that has helped to fill a lot of the other voids that were in my life. It's helped me build self-esteem. The spiritual side of my life has enhanced my whole life. When you're feeling down and depressed, pray and God lifts you up. I feel he has answered a lot of my prayers. I couldn't have made a lot of decisions or accomplishments in my life without the help of God.

I would like to continue my life helping kids to realize no matter where you start from you can always bring yourself up, especially kids and black females. Living here in Ontario, I'm kind of limited in reaching those particular minority children, so I just try to help any child I see needs the help or I can see were like me when I was a child. I try to help that child, talk to them. Sometimes, I tell them my life story to let them see, yes you can be somebody. You can realize a dream. If you set a course, if you set a goal, you can be somebody. You can accomplish it if you continue to work hard, believe and keep doing it step by step.

6

The Silent Roar of the Lion: Gregory's Story

Gregory is an African-American male in his forties. He is employed as a counselor in a program for at-risk students at a local community college. He is a man made thoughtful by years of struggling to reconcile the conflict emanating from a strong self-concept nurtured by his parents in his youth and a society that responded in ways that consistently challenged his perception of self. His is a story of struggling to come to terms with being black in a white world and his descent into antisocial behavior and ultimate triumph.

I was born in Mississippi. My father was from Greenville and my mother was from Jackson, Mississippi. They had the common work ethic that most Southerners had. They were hard workers. They believed you should live off the sweat of your brow and a person shouldn't want handouts. My father never went to school, and my mother went about as far as the eighth grade. My father was fifty and my mother was eighteen when I was born.

As I look back over my life, I look at it as being very unusual, and it had probably a lot of meaning in my overall attitude. I was prized highly by my father, being his first child at fifty years old. I was named after him. The story was told that he left Mississippi with me, came up North looking for a job, and later sent back for my mother and they started a family up here.

My father came North, I assume looking for work. The job he had up here was in a slaughterhouse. So, I assume he worked down there as an animal slaughterer or something of that nature. I was two years old when he brought me up here with him. I noticed my father had a good work ethic. I'm his junior; his nickname was "Go to Work" and he used to call me "Little Go to Work," because I liked to hang up under him. I remember he never took a vacation, and at that time you could take vacations, get your check and then go back to work and that's what he would do. I can remember that very plainly. I never remember him taking a day off from work unless he was sick.

His credibility was so strong, he could send back down for any of his relatives, his cousins, his nieces and bring them up here and a job was waiting for them. Eventually, we had a transplanted family unit up here. He would also find them a comfortable apartment in the area. Eventually, he sent for my mother's mother and my mother's sister and they lived with us. When it got too crowded, they would either get an apartment below, above or around the corner or something of this nature. We are very family-oriented. This is before the housing projects were built.

We were living in Chicago at this time. We came straight from Mississippi, right to where the projects are now at 43rd and State Street. From that particular point on, I think my life was very carefree and very loving. The whole household was loving. The neighborhood was loving. I remembered by me being the first child and being looked upon as the one that's going to make it, I was given a whole lot of room to grow. I knew right from wrong and I always tried to exhibit right in front of my parents, but I was just like most of the other children, very naughty, but I knew how to clean up my act in front of my parents. So, what I'm saying is, I was a model child from their perspective. That's what they needed, and that's what I gave them, because my parents worked hard. They both worked and grandmother usually watched the house. They trusted me and they really believed in my perception. They allowed me to hold conversations with them and express my opinion, which would have some outcome not only in my life but the life of my younger sisters and brothers. They engaged me in some of their business activities and things of this nature.

I remember wanting to emulate my father. I didn't understand what I wanted to emulate, but I wanted to emulate him. We had a coal stove. My father chopped wood, and I tried to chop wood in his absence. My father would give my mother money and she in return would give us little pennies, nickels and dimes. So, I would try to go out and hustle pop bottles to do the same thing for my sisters and brothers.

I remember wanting him to be a grandfather when I was very young and wanting to have a family, because he had a family. So, I went after that. The first time I tried to get a family, I asked my sister to adopt a child with me because I wanted to have a son. We wrote a letter and I remember the people writing back saying we were too young and it was very cute and all that kind of stuff. I had to be (about the time my father died) twelve years old.

As my father was dying, there was a young lady (a teenage girl) that used to hang with my sister. I had seven sisters and a cousin who was raised with us which we called our sister. So, there were eight girls in our household. She talked to my father a lot and attended to some of his needs, because we were kind of selfish. We were just running, running, running. We were, I guess, too young to realize what was going on, that he was dying. I thought, if she was socially acceptable to my father, she would be the person I would marry. So, I eventually asked her to marry me (at thirteen or fourteen years old) and everybody said I was crazy. But, I knew I was really set on it and so when we got to be fifteen, I went through the ritual of proposing. I think when I was about to turn seventeen, we came up with a scheme where our parents would have to let us get married and that was to have a child. So, we did the things you do to have a child and I knew it was a boy. I knew it was going to be my father's grandson, even though he wasn't alive. That was my primary preoccupation. I forgot about being a child a long time ago and of trying to please myself, my friends and my parents. That was always my primary goal, to please my parents but also be able to do what everybody else was doing. So, I eventually got my mother to let us get married. I eventually twisted her arm. She let us marry at seventeen. She had to sign for us. My son was going on his first year at that time. I stayed married for about fifteen years.

It never crossed my mind that I was poor, the way I was raised. I remember eating cornbread and milk for a meal or sugar sandwiches for a meal, not that I liked it but because that was all that was around. But, I really didn't realize I was poor until I got to be about thirty years old, because I was very happy and I was very content. I always felt my family provided within their means what I needed. I never saw any contradiction in that. I never saw them have what we didn't have, and I never saw us being short of anything and their having anything that was extravagant. So, therefore, I had no reason whatsoever to feel my parents were depriving me of anything. I did not feel that if I got a whipping it was anything wrong they were doing. As a matter of fact, I never got many whippings anyway. I got about two from my father in my whole life and maybe a dozen or so from my mother.

I had a lot of dreams, when I was young. My family allowed me to have these dreams. I had a lot of high expectations of myself. I was very arrogant and my family was very proud of the way I carried myself. When I was in third grade, my mother bought a TV and the man came in, a white man, and he was giving them some astronomical rates. I remember whining and crying and trying to be a man at the same time and told them that something was wrong. I was about eight years old. My father listened to me. I remember the man told him, "You're going to sit there and listen to that child," something like that. Anyway, they ended up signing the contract. Maybe two or three weeks later, my mother and father came up to me and said, "We should have listened to you. We should have had some other people look at some of the things in the contract."

I also remember at the age of eight, going to pay the bills for our various accounts. It was their lack of education. They trusted my development and growth and also my desire to be responsible and contribute to the family. There was a system we saw practiced by the family that the children emulated. As we grew up, it just fell in place. For instance, I knew my grandmother was the head of the house. I knew my father was next and my mother was next and I knew my auntie was next and then it was me, only because of age. I also noted within that hierarchy that my sister who was under me, was next and I would allocate to her what I couldn't do and then vice versa it would go all the way down. There were ten of us. I also saw what they did and we all tried to do the same thing.

I always wanted to please my parents, and they always said, education, education. So, that's one reason I was preoccupied with knowledge. From an educational point of view, I was very persistent when I started off. It's just that me and school had a conflict of interest and I was turned off by school from day one. My parents were believers in education and one of the things I heard from day one was you're going to go to school or work.

I was as clever as a child was going to get, because of the freedom my family allowed me. I transferred to three different high schools, forging my family's signature because I got in trouble and I didn't want my mother to take off from work because that to me was embarrassing. She worked too hard for the rest of my family; so, I just transferred myself out of schools to other schools and I could do that. I had that type of talent.

Then I also had a chance, in all fairness, to meet some teachers that were Southern oriented that probably took a liking to me, because I was one of the few kids that raised his hand when they asked were you born in Mississippi and I said I was. I remember some teachers even taught me how to court, date, mannerisms, behavior. All of the kind of stuff that was outside of the bounds of academics. But, I do know that my family allowed me to ask questions and sit down at the table with older people and inquire about whatever I wanted to. I don't want to confuse that, because I was not promiscuous in my sexual development. I did not go outside the realms of the normal social code of the day, but I do remember when I went to school, I felt like I was being stifled.

I emulated my father so much, a lot of times the children would jump on me at school or the teacher would have them harass me, because I would sneak my father's hat, shoes, tie out and just before I got to school, I would put them on. I just wanted to wear them. I was different, but I wasn't aware that I was different. It wasn't I was different because I was awkward, physically disproportionate or disrespectful, because I'm very mannerable to this day. I just think I had a belief that was contrary to what I saw.

I remember I had to see a psychiatrist quite a few times in school. The first time I had to see the psychiatrist was when I was in kindergarten or first grade, when I was asked the question, "What's the difference between mamma bear and papa bear?" I remember it was kind of funny with the family, because I got a whipping about it because I said, mamma had titties. So, they called my mother and they said I was jesting. They brought a psychiatrist in and they said what's the answer supposed to be. The answer was supposed to be the father bear was the biggest. That was supposed to be the answer but in my house, my mother was much bigger than my father. My mother was twice as big as my father. The only association I could see was that I was breast fed. The only association I could see, I guess at the time, was the fact that she had titties and he didn't. That's when my tag or label came in.

My parents whipped me for being unruly in school, because usually when I read or something, I was disciplined for not wanting to give the answer the teachers wanted. This caused my parents to have to come to the school for delinquent behavior. That was my first encounter with school that I really didn't like besides being teased and chased when I wore my father's clothes.

I was, basically, encountering white teachers. I remember Miss Swanson. She was my principal. But basically, they were white teachers. I really had my critics, but my parents always supported the school. Even though they gave me my freedom, they always felt that particular segment of society was correct. That's where my conflict of interest was at that point. I could not please my family anymore, if I was messing up in school.

In fifth or sixth grade, we were asked what we wanted to be and I still had this air about myself that I was going to be a great contributor to my people, to my family and make everybody proud of me. I was looking at the world and I was picking up on some of the prejudices at this particular point in time. I think this was also about the time I went to Emmett Till's funeral. They had his funeral up here in Chicago and there was a big story on it, because he was killed near my home town, but he was from Chicago and they had the funeral up here right across the street from my house and we had to go. He was killed for supposedly whistling at a white woman.

The church was on 41st and State where everybody went to view his body. I remember being asked, "What do you want to be?" I remember being scared for the first time, very scared. I remember giving it a whole lot of thought and I said, the vice president of the United States. In my heart, I wanted to be the president, but I was too scared to say that. That was the only time I ever believed I couldn't be it. That was the first time I really looked at it and said, you know, you really can't be the president, and with the feedback I was getting in school, well. So, now I wanted to be the vice president, or a senator or a teacher and from that point on I was told you should rather be a teacher. You can't be this and you can't be that.

The white counselors told me this. They were saying I was wasting my time thinking about that. Being a teacher was about all I could be. I really looked at being a teacher as something I could do to help my race and our society as a whole, because I figured if I helped us (and I felt that we were in the worst position in this structure) it would make the whole structure better. I was feeling good about some of these things. You have to realize this is going back to feeling good about pleasing my father. This was before he died.

I was going to be one of the greatest athletes in the world, because I remember playing with him as a child and I remember him playing catch with me. I'm looking at him and seeing that he couldn't keep up with me, because he's getting older and older and he was broken down, but he always tried to interact with me. I could see that he liked sports. He would talk about Willie Mays and Ernie Banks. I said if he likes them, I like them. So, this is what he liked, this is what I'm going to be. So, as a kid, I started excelling in athletics. I was very, very good in every sport I attempted. If I didn't make the first team, I wouldn't quit until I did. When the realization of his death came to me, everything just seemed to have a different slant.

The point I'm trying to make is, within my family structure, I cannot see any deficiency that would have caused me to go off the way I did. Matter of fact, the thing that brought me back was the concept of a good mother and a good father. When things hit rock bottom in my life, they were the focus point. Your father did not work that hard for you to be this. Your mother would not approve of this. But for all practical purposes, all the guidance, all of the ingredients, the love and the care, it was there.

The opportunities were there. I just felt I was disillusioned and not able to handle the realization that I was in a world where color had a lot to do with how we act. I had been well trained to that. I think that's a part of the "yes ma'am" and "no ma'am." I think that's why my parents taught me at a very young age the Southern concept of being respectful, so you won't be questionable in interacting with white people in the South. But, the realization of a black and white world was not as harmful as the realization that black folks seemed to be ashamed of being black and I didn't have enough role models around, at a young age, to emulate that pride that I had.

You have to realize, I was kind of arrogant and when I read the Bible, I saw some of the prophets and angels as black people. How I got that particular concept I don't know, but as I got older, I was not able to keep those perceptions intact, because then I started getting into more formalized religion, more orthodox religions where the books would color code white. The doctrines always emulated those characteristics as being positive. But, society didn't allow me that. It didn't allow me to look at this kind of hair as being OK, but I was already fixed, so I couldn't have any other kind of hair. It was forcing values on me that I didn't like and that I was ashamed of and scared of. All of the positive strokes I used to get were changing. I had to like light-skinned women, not because they were women but because they were light-skinned. That's the way I was feeling.

By me being the oldest of ten children, I always had a way of wanting to take care of the less fortunate. I started to find out that you shouldn't be looking out for other people, you should utilize your strength and power to deprive and take, to monopolize. Most of my life, I didn't have that as a stimulus. I was more encouraged and caressed for the group activities I was brought up in, because of my family household. But, the friends I chose to take up with were beginning to be considered outcasts, as we got older. They were usually the slower kids.

My reasons for wanting things got to be a little different. I loved my first marriage because I thought we got married because we were going to do things together and it was going to be us. I had relationships outside of my first marriage, and after my first marriage. The difference was what you can do for me, whereas in my first marriage it was what are we going to do. I just felt like I was really lost, and the only other institution that I saw that could enhance what I would like was Christianity. But, it was losing me, because as far as I was concerned (I'm a very sensitive person too) it was still highlighting white features to me.

My grandmother was a minister and she was deeply involved in the church and Jesus Christ. One of the pastimes I spent with my grandmother was, she would read me biblical stories. They were very interesting, not from a religious point of view to me, but from a historical perspective. My mother told me about the story of Samson and Delilah. I read it all in the Bible, but now I'm getting to look at it on motion picture and they're all white. Cleopatra and everything come out white, and it's almost like all of my peers and all of my family and everybody else I wanted to be around are saying this is true, and even if it isn't true, you're foolish for wanting to be black anyway. This is what I thought I was feeling and what I was hearing.

Then the black movement came in and that gave me a reprieve. Again, during the 60s, I remember most of the teenagers and some of the adults had the perception that we were special, because now we were allowed to highlight things I thought should have been highlighted in the first place, like wearing robes, dashikis, afros and things of this nature—being natural. I think after the killing of Fred Hampton, the destroying of the Black Panther Party and a lot of other stuff that came down, blacks as well as whites systematically accepted it.

But acceptance was not my problem. I'd been accepting things all my life. But, we also justified it. I was always taught that two wrongs don't make a right. Yet and still I saw society doing something equally as bad to the "wrongdoers," because they didn't demonstrate their particular beliefs or disapproval in the proper manner. Society still dealt with them with another wrong. I think at this particular point in time, I started going to drugs and that's when my life took a turn.

We're talking about several things happening. When I descended into drugs, we're talking about experimental and then actual escapism. I think I was seventeen when I actively started experimenting with drugs. I think when I got to be about twenty-one or twenty-two, I was completely using drugs as a release, as an escape. I felt that was the best way I could deal with my situation, because that way my world became the same as it was when I was a child and I could see the things that I enjoyed better. I could read a book and I could hallucinate and fantasize and get into a particular perspective that I wanted to see and it was still under control. I still had that protectiveness of all of my friends, my associates and my family. At the same time, everything started deteriorating. I, eventually, lost my wife and had no direction. I had nothing to hold onto and if it wasn't for my mother and a little bit of trying to hide stuff from her, that's what stopped me from going off the deep end.

However, I remember being revived on jobs that I have had where I overdosed in the men's room and they had to call an ambulance. I don't know how I called myself trying to keep it away from her. It got to the point where I really didn't care. So, it reached a climax. Then a lot of the real drug users, heavier users than me, took me in because I was one of them. They were taking in a nice resource, because I was creative. So, my talents went from wanting to be a leader of my people to being a provider of drugs for the people I was with. Three-fourths of my energy went to not just supplying a high for myself, but for supplying a high for the group that I attached myself to. I still had that protective factor. But, there's no way you're going to be on drugs and not offend or affect the people that you love. I didn't steal from my folks or anything like that.

I never violated anybody black in getting the money. As a matter of fact, I got to the point where I used to tear up money. My sisters and brothers still tease me about that to this day. I would just tear it up, because I still was not enchanted with anything I was doing. I was still rebelling against a social system that placed great value on a materialistic existence. I would take all the money just to buy highs for the group. I would also put a levy on them too. You come up with a hundred, I'll give five or something like that to make it challenging for me, because I enjoyed that.

I would do things like raid warehouses, set up burglaries in some of the small jewelry shops in the area, railroad hijacking (not the train itself but the cars and trucks), things like that. We set up things where we would give other people money. I just liked to feel like I was kind of like Robin Hood or something. We'd give it to people that we knew. They were not criminals. They just needed some money. They could have been students going to school and needed books or something. It was a great honor for me to feel I was still needed and I was providing.

Also, my word was still good. I always kept my word with the people I associated with, whether I was on drugs or not. I could be counted on. I like being part of a team. Plus, I liked the idea of being counted on. I got that from my family with my ten sisters and brothers. I enjoyed that. To this day, I still enjoy doing things, from the agape point of view. I like trying to do as much as I can without an ulterior motive. I feel better about myself when I'm like that and that group was that outlet.

I remember one time we were arguing over who was going to get to shoot the drugs first. I'm looking at the group (there's nothing you can do with a bunch of grown men and everybody wants to go first), so, I said, we'll split it up like this and I split it up into different size segments and said whoever went first would get the smallest segment and so forth. I don't care who goes first, but the smallest amount is going to be used first. So, everybody wanted to be last and that became the mode. That was very unusual in a group for everybody to want to be last. It seemed like everybody was being compliant, were considerate. A drug addict likes to get his kick off right away. That group gave me a chance to be that type of person. It's just that after a while, I guess you could say, psychologically, my discipline was beginning to go. I'm talking about my discipline as far as tolerance.

Noise began to bother me and arguments began to have a real profound effect on me. I was not able to restrain myself and so I began getting more hostile and more violent and that's when the crime started. That's when my trouble started and I didn't even care. I got involved in a murder case and I pleaded guilty because I knew I was wrong. But the State saw probable cause and gave me four years probation. I thought that was bad. I almost killed somebody, but the State gave me four years for that and I pleaded guilty. I said I was wrong but they still just gave me four years. Again, that justified my feeling that they couldn't care less about African-Americans, because the crime I committed was against blacks. So anyway, I didn't go to jail.

I stayed out for two years on that. I was still on drugs and I was getting busted. It got to the point where I didn't even care and I would just say "Yes, they're mine" and tell the judge that I'm not killing nobody, I'm not stealing, I'm not doing nothing wrong, I'm just getting high. I can do whatever I want with my life, leave me alone. And they never would send me to prison, never.

Then, I decided I wanted to change my life around and somebody told me, "You're wasting your life." So, I put myself in a couple of programs, but that didn't work out. So, I started trying to develop my education and they got me for probation. I failed to come to see my probation officer and that's what they sent me to jail for, not coming to see my probation officer. But, I did see him.

By this time, I didn't want to go to jail, because I was trying to change my life around. I remember having a traumatic feeling that it's really happening to me. At this point, you have to realize they were saying I violated my probation. But, I wasn't scared or anything because this was the one time, after all the bad I'd done in my life, I had straightened myself out. I went to school and I had gotten a job with the largest advertising agency in the world. I was thinking about getting into white American. I really was. I was thinking about becoming an entrepreneur; white people liking me. Now, I had all of these credentials, but I was still going to court because I had violated my probation.

I went before the judge and I had the people from the company come there and they wrote letters. I had people from the school writing letters, ministers and everybody wrote letters about the remarkable turnaround I had made within the last three or four months. So, the prosecutor said, "Well, you're just doing this so you won't go to prison." Then my lawyer said, "If that's what he's doing it for, that's good. We should have more people like that."

So, anyway the judge said, "Is there anybody else you want to have testify? You want to have your mother?" So, I said, "No, go on and give me the sentence." I really didn't think I was going to go to prison because I saw so much wrongdoing that went unpunished. The judge said, "You want to come back tomorrow?" and I said no, just tell me what you're going to do. He said, we're going to reopen your case and give you three to six and I really thought he was joking just to see if I was going to get angry or something. So, I went back to the lockup and my lawyer came back and said, "You know you're doing three to six, but you'll be able to take off about a year or two." I saw myself getting angry at my lawyer but then after that, I realized I was going to jail for three years.

I went to prison and I realized I was going to be there and I started doing the next best thing and that was (as most people do), I started getting back close to my religious roots. But, I wouldn't allow myself to ask God for forgiveness. I just tried to acknowledge the wrong I did and try to accept the punishment and try to do better for God in the future. I was working with some men in prison and they were working with me trying to get me to convert. I was already converted but they wanted me to ask God to give me something I wouldn't ask for before I got in trouble. I thought that was less than a man also. But these guys would pray with me and we would talk and everything.

They were inmates too, you know. They were doing much more time than I was doing and a lot of guys also knew me from the streets. So, I didn't have that outside danger a lot of people had coming in there. A lot of them believed (the ones that hadn't seen me for years) that I was the kid that was going to be the great baseball player, or doctor or lawyer. They couldn't imagine me being incarcerated. But because of the love and respect for the type of person they knew I was, they buffered me from possible danger. Later, I realized that was God protecting me.

Events happened that I don't know how they happened. I don't know if somebody was trying to set me up, but I came to my cell one day and there was a whole lot of knives and stuff in there. They said, the guys said for you to keep your mouth shut. Don't tell anybody about it. I told them, "Well you know, I'm not going to leave this in my cell. So, I turned them in to the guard and then some other stuff happened.

During this period of time, my family would come visit, my mother, my sister and my auntie. I got tired of seeing them, because I finally realized I was finding myself. I asked my mother not to come and see me anymore. I told my mother, no I was just content and I understand what's going on with myself and I'm not going to be here long anyway. Even though I was scheduled to do three to six years, I was just about on my sixth month and for some reason or another, I had the feeling that I was going to get out.

I prayed to God in my own little way and I did acknowledge what I should be about, and a dream came to me. It told me that I was going home on September something, go back to school. That's what you should do. I told my mother to get things ready, and everybody thought I was crazy. I think it was August 14th when this particular school started back. I didn't know then, but I got out August 13th and I was ready to go to school on the 14th.

When I came home, I had all these big ideas. This was back in 1980. I started drugs in '67. In prison, I had a habit of watching TV and changing channels, so I would not see sensuous things. I got into stuff like Clint Eastwood movies with these shoot-em-ups and things like that. I remember seeing a lot of food commercials, and I never had a desire or inkling for steaks and lobsters but that was the first thing I said I was going to do when I got out. I said I wasn't going to get high, but I eventually did get high and looked for some of the guys and my female friends because I had a little cash.

I went in with cash, because I used to do a lot of things and one of my biggest scams before I went in was accident swindles. I used to get into phony accidents about three or four a year. You'd get a settlement of about $6,000 or $7,000 each after the lawyer took out all his money. I was hooked up with the white man in doing this. So, it wasn't like I'm doing something wrong because this is what was taught to me. It was another avenue of hustling. So, I had that money all ready for me when I came out. I got some friends together and the next thing, I was getting high and I started drinking.

I hated alcohol. I never liked it. I was an athlete. One thing about an athlete, you don't drink. But, I was around people who drank, and not only was I getting high on heroin, but coke was the acceptable high when I got out of prison, cocaine. So, I wanted to be with the highs. I wanted to be accepted. So, I started doing coke. I started speedballing. That was mixing coke and heroin together. But when I got around people I started drinking, putting alcohol on my lips and tongue, developing a front that I was a drunkard. I started freebasing with crack and stuff. This was about '82 or '83, about two or three years after prison.

I was working odds and ends jobs. I wasn't hustling like I use to. I was very disciplined. What I mean by this is, I was living within my means, but I utilized the system. I was drawing unemployment, getting welfare checks and working parttime all at the same time, to try to support my habit. Plus, I was going to school under different names and getting loans. They hadn't cracked down on that real hard—getting the PELL grants.

I remembered looking at everything around me and I still was looking at the children and seeing that they were going nowhere. They are really going nowhere. And I remember seeing cruel games being played and then it dawned on me what my mother always talked about. What about being a teacher and a minister. I would see her every once in a while, and she kept talking about that. She went back down South to live and then she developed cancer and she came up here to be near her family to die.

Just before I went to prison, my mother had a stroke. It was in her restaurant. She had her own restaurant and I was like the manager of the restaurant. I took care of everything, the books and all that kind of stuff. I was in the bathroom getting high and I overdosed. Everybody was trying to tell her what kind of son she had, you know, to bust her bubble. I looked around and could see her whole face had just twisted up and it stayed like that. That happened in '76.

It stayed like that while I was in prison. When she came back from down South, she lived with us the rest of her life. That was about '87 or '88. I was still looking at my mothers face all twisted. So, I started to tell my mother I was going to change, because she kept saying, You ought to have your own school and teach and do this and do that. That's why I started to tell my mother I was going to do that. This came to me when I got out of prison.

Then I got a job as a teacher's aide. I was telling the children about not getting high. I had just gotten over my drug addiction, but I was using alcohol as a disguise to help get me out of other situations. I remember going to the store to get some alcohol, and a couple of kids came in, and I remember feeling guilty. These were athletes too. So, I asked for the alcohol and the guy put it on the counter and these kids came up right behind me, and I walked away from the alcohol. They said, Didn't you ask for this, and I said, No, I didn't ask for that. So, I got some juice or pop or something.

I went out of the store and waited until the kids left. When they left, I went back into the store and asked the guy for the alcohol again, and the kids came in again. I told the guy I didn't ask for it again. He told me to get my crazy butt out the store. At that point in time, I knew I had to either love them (the kids) or love that. These were kids I had been talking to, but I didn't know personally.

So, I went back to my mother and we talked. She told me she was dying. I remember all this hit me, the dreams, the values we talked about when I was younger. The things she was trying to reintegrate into my being were more important than my high. I remember saying to my mother (this was in '86) I was going to stop getting high and I did basically. I really stopped getting high basically and I went back to school and graduated.

When I graduated, my mother was in the hospital. She lived about a week or two after that and her face twisted back. This is the God's truth. When I came with my cap and gown into the hospital room, I had to take a picture with her. I told her I had quit drugs, and I was now on my third year not doing anything and I was thinking about the ministry. I was going to work with young people. That's where I am now.

The other thing that happened in '86, I was telling my supervisor I was going to quit. I remember I said I was going to get full of it. I said I was going to do everything before I quit on New Year's. This was December 26th, I think. I remember saying, I really want to quit this time. I think about from the 28th, every day, I was buying as much as I could, to get as high as I could. I didn't care what it was, because on the 1st I'm going to quit. On the 28th, I just fell out, out of exhaustion. I was going to sleep and something said, "If you really want to quit on January 1st, you want to quit now. This is the God's truth. Something said, You will never, ever have a need to smoke, drink, get high, gamble or curse again." From that point on in '86 to this day, that's what's happened. I haven't smoked or used drugs. I have no desire or need to ever do any of those things again.

I do feel the love of my race and the children is much more important to me than the high. It's even more important than the ego. I feel my ego was also part of my reasons for escaping. My ego would not allow me to, gracefully, humbly accept the plight I was in as a black man. Not as an individual, as a black man, and look for honorable means to work with it. At this particular point in my life,

I'm trying to control my ego, and I do believe through the Word, through religion there's a way to combat the problems I felt I had no other way to deal with.

As a child coming up, my values were good values. What I saw was good. Now, I tried to teach that it's one thing having these things and not to have them control you. I didn't understand that and that was my confusion. It's one thing having a Cadillac and having it control you. It's one thing having a house and having it control you. It's one thing having a wife and having her control you. I saw those things as me, my worth. If you live life and never have a car, you know it shouldn't be your worth. It's only a vehicle or instrument to enhance you. I think when I reached that realization, I was able to deal with society from a different perspective. Now, I'm able to see that there is a rainbow for us as a people.

If I had to sum it up, that's what I call success, that other people's behavior and actions do not have a total or dominant effect on my happiness or feelings. I don't think anyone is successful, if you can't help another in some way. I don't care how rich or poor you are, if you're not able to really help another then you're not successful, and I don't mean monetarily.

I had to get out of this pity thing. I could justify anything I saw. I was in an organization where I was called the Minister of Propaganda. So, its easy to take a situation and cry and lean on it. I think my biggest difficulty was to accept facts for what they were and try to work with it. There are a lot of reasons, social conditions that, justifiably so, put young black men in that situation, but that shouldn't be the crux of their whole life.

Television, the media and even some of our people in authority paint a picture of success without ever opening up legitimate doors of achievement. When I was a kid, the most famous movie was the Mack and this was before I got into drugs. I had two friends younger than me, two fifteen-year-olds, that immediately went into drug dealing and came up with the exact car that the Mack had in the movie. It was the Cadillac with the red and whites. This is the God's truth. They had the coat and everything. The point that I'm getting at is, the media and society paint a picture of where you should be to be accepted but they never show people positive ways of getting there. The only means they show of getting there is negative.

The first Air Jordan commercial, for example. They had Spike Lee talking to this girl. And the girl said, "You're a square, don't talk to me, get away from me." He went and put on some Air Jordan shoes, and she fell in his arms. This has an effect on a child. They are very impressionable and they really believe this. What I'm trying to say is, if we as a society are going to paint a picture of materialistic needs to be accepted, then we should also paint a picture of positive ways to achieve this goal.

Our children never see that. They are not exposed to civil service jobs. They don't know that if they graduate from school at twenty-one and work until they are fifty-five, they would have made more than a half million dollars. They don't understand those figures. They are not taught that with the proper discipline, the proper investment, they have the potential to be millionaires. The only outlets I see, basically, geared to African Americans are quick money and robberies.

I had nobody I could talk to in my life that was something like a mentor. A person that goes before you that has worked up from the bottom to the top. I don't have that now. I have people in my life that are of that stature, but I didn't have them as role models when I was growing up. When my father died, I was not completely isolated from male figures or male role models. My minister had a very active role in being concerned about my mother's children. The teachers and the police department in the neighborhood where I grew up had an active concern. When my father died, I went on a rampage. I was discontent with anger and hate. But, I was not arrested because the police in the area, at that particular time, knew about my father's death. We weren't just a number in the community.

I don't think too many people had a negative effect on me. I just think I was what I was. There were people that had a positive effect on me. There were a couple of teachers that had a definite approach and had a positive impact on me. I know that they were good role models. I remember one guy. The last time I saw him was in 1966 and I called him last year in January which was 1992. That's how profound he was. He was like a recruiter to get an education to get into radio and TV. He was a radio announcer for a sportscaster and I told him why he had a profound effect on me. He had even forgotten me and I thought nobody could forget me. I used to love this man so much, I would do wrong just to hear him holler at me. I'd make stupid mistakes and out of all the mistakes and all the wrong I would do, he would turn around and say, "Jesus Christ," you know, like that. He would never swear. He would never lose his temperament. I mean I would do some stuff to irk him on purpose. He was my basketball coach in high school.

His name was James Hartman. He played for the university. He played on their national championship team in '61 or '62. He was an overachiever. But, I remembered just like seeing him smile. He never cursed and it didn't look like he drank or smoked. He didn't look like he gambled. He didn't tell locker room jokes or jokes about women and all that kind of stuff. He was just unbelievable.

If I could live my life again, I don't think I would be cracking jokes on women. I don't think I would be cursing. I don't think I would be drinking or doing stupid stuff. I think people can do that. I believe to this day that he did it, because that was what I saw. By far, he stands out in my life probably more so than anybody, except for my father. There were other people that I got close to that had a positive effect on me but not as much as him, because I saw their flaws, their way of life. Whereas my coach was different. A teacher should not be a companion. Our children have enough friends. I mean like if I was a teacher, I shouldn't turn around and then ask a guy, let's go to a party and all this kind of stuff. I think he has that. He has enough of that. With my coach, I'm not saying when I got older, I would not have appreciated going out with him. But, I appreciate the distance he kept there at that age, because I was growing up anyway and he set boundaries that there is a difference between a man and you. If he had allowed me, I wouldn't have developed and grown. That's what I think a mentor is.

There was one teacher that taught me how to date. She used to make fun of me. She was a black teacher. I used to dislike her. I disliked her passionately. I knew I had a good family and my parents were good. A lot of times, I would come in from playing and would go straight to sleep with the intention of washing up the next morning. But, I'd oversleep, because I watched TV real late and went out the house without really washing up and still had the smudge of dirt form the day before. The teacher would always make remarks about that. I thought she was putting me down. She would bring me in front of the class and say stuff like, "Girls, would you like a man like this" and all that kind of stuff, and my feelings would be hurt. I remember saying, "I'm going to get her." So, I went home that night and I scrubbed and scrubbed and looked at TV like I normally did. I stayed up a little late and got up the next morning, because I was intending to wash up again the next morning too, you know. But, I was running late as usual and I ran on to school. I got to school and she called me in front of the classroom. I said, "Oh man, here we go again" (I forgot that I bathed the night before).

She called me up and she looked and she said, "Class look at him, isn't this a nice young man; isn't he a pretty young man?" She said, "You got up and washed your face this morning." I said, "No, I didn't." Which I didn't, and I was trying to hurt her some more. I said, "No, I didn't." She said, "An angel came and washed it." I said, "It must have." I had forgotten that I had washed it that night. But, I liked that attention. So, I started doing that. Eventually, I got closer to her and she would give me books to read about what a gentleman should do. I was in fifth or sixth grade. What you should do on a date and all. I think it was called *Teenager*.

I knew she genuinely cared. She would even talk to my mother. She would come by and visit my house and talk to my mother. Even though I had a behavior problem to a degree, I was always getting good grades (at least the grades that I wanted to get) and she would emphasize that. She would let my mother know I was a bright child and a child to be proud of and I was a very smart student.

She was plain, not a lot of makeup, not a lot of up-to-do hair dos, homely like clothes, but there was more. I didn't see her like children see teachers today. I could see beyond the lack of glamor, because of the way she carried herself. That was a positive experience. A very positive experience.

The other teacher I had in the third grade was also black. She would spank me. After she spanked me, she would make me kiss her. She would make all the children she spanked kiss her. I associated discipline with truth and trust and this particular teacher would do that. She would make us kiss each other. It was almost like she was using reverse psychology. We became an entity to her and not just a stump, because she had to get to each person's head. I don't see that anymore with teachers. I see we are gladly trying to push everybody into one unified conglomerate to make our job easier. The teachers I'm talking about treated you as individuals and they were respected for that. They encouraged you with things that stimulated you. That's how I see education. That's what I got from the people I'm talking about. White teachers didn't have that particular perspective most of the time.

Another teacher I really hated, but I love to this day, I can't remember her name but she was a gray-haired teacher who wore glasses. She made us speak Spanish in second grade. She was a black teacher. Most of the teachers I'm talking about were Southern. They were all from the South and I know they were from the South, because we would talk about these sort of things. This is not to say Northern teachers did not have the interest or concern and care, but I think at that time most of the people in the South were getting degrees in education and coming up North looking for jobs. It was very unique to see her take a half an hour or two out of the day to put in the curriculum something that was not part of the curriculum, because she saw the need of us having a second language. I did not continue with it and the school did not continue it. But again, I think about the dislike that I had for her, because I felt she forced that down my throat. But you know, that was just her way. She spanked our hands too. I know you can't do that anymore.

In grade school, I didn't have that much contact with males. I had mostly females. I can't remember any males in grade school. In high school, I had the coach. I guess the only other person that was of an educational value as a mentor or anything else was another coach at another high school. But they were all coaches. These guys were still people that didn't curse and they had a way of setting limits. They treated you like you were something. But, I don't have to kiss your butt to make you a part of what we are. I want you, but you should want to be here just as much as we want you here or it's no relationship. It was not a thing that they would bend over backwards to wheel you in, but by no means were they inviting you out.

Sports kept me out of trouble. It really did. Sports kept me in school. When I got angry or had a problem, even a math problem, I would go out and play basketball or something like that by myself and then I would come back and look at the problem and it was easier to deal with.

David Sharpe was another very positive person in my life because of his success. I saw him as a person who was striving to maintain a level of integrity. I didn't like him when I first met him. I thought he was an Uncle Tom. I thought he was hand-fed. I thought he never had any problems in life, no hardships, no adversities. Therefore, I thought he shouldn't be liked. After meeting him, I strived to want to get into civic matters, because I saw him do things he didn't have to do. It's not always the people who have it hard that have the sensitivity, that's what I'm trying to get at. There are people that don't have it hard that have sensitivity. They might not understand everything that goes on, but he showed me that you can be successful and sensitive. You can have integrity.

I looked at him and he taught me that crying is not the way to solve your problems. Sometimes when I was coming up, I thought crying was the best way to start solving a problem, because now you're going to get some pity and people will make it a little easier for you than it was before. He reminded me of what my parents talked about. He used to talk about people didn't like the idea that you had to be twice as good to go half as far and that's what I saw in David. Even though people called him Uncle Tom, and I thought he was one too, I saw him not using the saying that if I wasn't black I wouldn't have to work so hard. So his behavior had an effect on me, even now.

One of the things, when I think about my mother dying, was the love she and my father had for me. This would be a key to success. I remember my mother was the matriarch that had everybody's welfare at heart. I could look in her eyes and tell by the way she talked and the way she acted that she had a game plan that would encompass all that you would encounter. I think my success with my children would be to make sure they would all be happy. They only way I know they can be happy is that they gain a certain amount of knowledge, a certain perspective and values that would not be altered or swayed by other people's interpretation, thinking or action or inaction. If a person can actually take the worst thing that could happen to them and see that as an event, but not their life, I think everything else comes with that. That's what I consider success.

7

No Restrictions, No Convictions: Carole's Story

Carole is a woman in her early fifties. She exudes a vibrance and energy that is contagious. She speaks with the assuredness of one who knows exactly who she is and how she came to be. Her stature projects a strong sense of pride and confidence. It is ironic that she credits her positive attributes to her will and determination to overcome the emotional scars of years of childhood sexual abuse and never to be victimized again.

My mom did domestic work and my father was a common laborer. After my sister was born, my mom and dad separated and later divorced. I understand that my father's mother wanted me and my sister to live with her. There was a court battle. My grandmother on my mother's side had to go to court to say she would be responsible for me and my sister. At this particular time, we were living in Chicago Heights, but my mother was born and raised in a little town in the South. I had to be about two years old, when my parents divorced.

I knew very little about my father. My grandfather, my mother's father, was my father image; that's who I looked up to. I lived with just my grandmother, because my grandparents were divorced. My mother was hardly ever home. My mother's sister was a beautician, and she did my hair. She lived in the same town. The lifestyle my mother led was not becoming where she could bring it into the home. The only thing I know is, she always brought us real pretty clothes. I remember when I was real small, she used to give me a bath and put me in a chair, stand me up in a chair so I wouldn't get dirty or mess up my petticoat or anything like that. I got all the teaching from my grandmother. It was she that I watched cook the gingerbread and little things and tell me to stay in school.

She was a person that believed in obeying your elders. I remember the "yes ma'am and the "no ma'am." She embedded that in me. I took piano lessons, and that was one thing I did not like. The music teacher lived next door and my grandmother said, "You have to do this, because whatever you get in your head, no one can ever take that away from you. It's always best to know more than one thing to do." I never understood that, until I got older. Another thing she used to always say to me was, we as a race of people will have it very hard anyway, because of our color.

My grandmother and mother did domestic work. They went to white people's homes and cleaned. I remember times when they would bring back some of their clothing. There were times when I used to help my mom and my grandmother with some of the holidays the Jewish people had. I had to go in their homes to help them, and it was a little extra money for me to make also. I did that even as a little girl, eleven or twelve years old. I waited on tables and cleaned their homes, and I knew I didn't want to do that.

I can remember as a twelve-year-old girl, when they had their Jewish Hanukkah, I would go with my grandmother and help her prepare the food and tidy up afterwards. I learned a little bit about their culture, but I got paid for that. I knew that wasn't what I wanted. I used to always say to my grandmother, "How could you come in and clean up their dirty dishes, cook their food and pick things off the floor?" I knew I could not do that. I didn't like doing it at home, why should I do it for somebody else. I especially didn't like that I had to go around to the back door. We weren't allowed to come through the front door. I couldn't understand that, but you didn't ask any questions. So, I knew I didn't like that.

There were a couple of incidents where my mom or grandmother would get sick and they would say to me, "You will have to go to Mrs. Brachmeyer today for me because I'm not well." I was about fifteen years old. I remember going, and she wanted to compare me with my grandmother. I didn't like that, because I was my own person and the way she might have done things, I might have done differently. I got yelled at, and I didn't like that. It was the tone of Mrs. Brachmeyer's voice, and the way she acted, "You must do what I say do. If I tell you to do it like Anna, then that's the way I want it to be done." I didn't like that. I always knew I didn't want to work for anyone. I want to have my own business.

My grandmother used to always tell me, "In order for you to not have to do what I'm doing or your aunt or your mother, you've got to get your education, and that's the only way. Being black and female, you've got to go to school." I ended up being a high school drop-out, getting pregnant and marrying my children's father and having very low self-esteem. The marriage went sour, and I never thought about Carole until the divorce and then I knew I wanted more out of life. I wanted to have a home, beautiful clothes and a car, the whole bit. I did not want to work for nobody for forty hours a week. In order for me to do that, I picked up on what my grandmother had said, go back to school.

Because my mother and grandmother worked out, as a child, I knew we had to have that house cleaned, and I knew we had to have dinner started. That was my chore. The house had to be cleaned, the dinner had to be started, and clothes had to be washed on a Friday. I was given these responsibilities at about eleven years old. We were disciplined.

I was one that like to go to socials. At that time, they called the little house parties "socials." Someone would have it in their basement, and we'd pay a quarter to get in. They called it "blue light socials." I was forbidden to go to them. I came from a very religious family, and only bad girls went to the little parties where they only had a blue light showing, and you didn't know where they were going to be. They knew what was going on. They knew about the slow dancing and the whole bit, and young girls at that time were still getting pregnant. So, my grandmother said only bad girls go to that. So, I was forbidden to go, but all my friends were going and they would tell me about it. I would pretend like I was in bed and sneak out. I would climb out the window and go. That's how I was able to go to the blue light socials.

I, eventually, got caught. My sister and I had this little conflict, so she told my grandmother and my grandmother was waiting for me when I came back through the window that night. I never will forget. She took a skillet (at that time they used the old black iron skillets) and gave me a good whipping with that skillet. Then, I got reprimanded the next day by my grandfather.

I was taken to his house, and at the time, they had the post beds where the headboards had posts on them. He took his razor belt (because I was a runner, I would run) and tied my hands to one of the posts. He got three switches from the backyard, skinned them, braided them like you braid a little girl's hair and that's what I got a whipping with.

At the time, I resented my grandparents for the severe discipline. I remember telling my grandmother, "I honestly hate you for doing me this way" and she said, "You know what, one day you're going to thank me. You may not see it now, but you're going to became a parent one day and then you're going to understand why I'm doing all of this."

Believe me, I understood it, because two of my sons practically nailed me to the cross. I remember going to one of the Catholic schools they were in. Sister called me on the job and told me Tony was upsetting the class. He was the class clown. I had to work, and I got so sick and tired of Sister calling me and telling me I had to leave work and come over, I gave him a spanking, an old-fashioned whipping in front of the class, with his pants down. A lot of things my grandmother told me came to pass, being a mother. At that particular time, parents could do that. Parents, I understand, can't do that now. You don't embarrass your child, otherwise you may find yourself dead.

I was molested as a child by a family member. It gave me strength. I could never tell that, because when he did this to me, it was "You can never tell this." I was about eight years old. It happened about three years before I started my period. I was safe to him, because I couldn't get pregnant. He instilled in my mind, I couldn't say anything about it because everybody would say I was a bad girl. I would be the cause of it. Some kind of way, it would be my fault. That's one of the reasons I couldn't say anything about this. That's what he told me, and I believed it. It made me very hard, when it came to men, and along with the teaching my grandfather instilled in me, it made me harder. It was always a thing, I don't need you to tell me what I have to do. I don't need you to take care of my needs. If you can't supply these particular things, I don't need you.

The sexual abuse continued for about five years. It eased off, once I started having my periods. He had a peculiar odor. It wasn't a musty or foul odor, it was not that cologne men use when they shower or shaving lotion, but there was a peculiar odor. Even after he died, I could smell him in my sleep. I could smell him when I had sex with my husband. It took God to remove a lot of that, and it took me talking about it to remove a lot of things.

I talked to my third son about it, because he's gay. I had to, for me to understand him and to let him know that you're not born that way. I wanted to know if anything happened to him as a child, and it had. The same pervert also did it to him.

What started the conversation between us was, he insulted my intelligence by saying he believed he was born that way. There are too many scriptures in the Bible that let us know that's not true. So, for me to really dig deep into what he was all about, I had to go back to my childhood to let him know what had happened to me. It could have resulted in that same situation, but it was just through the grace of God that I didn't. I went the route of wanting to prove something, wanting to be more, and to let men know I really didn't need them. I don't need you to take care of me. I don't need you to have me as your little piece of meat whenever you want to have sex, as if that's all I'm for.

When I was molested as a child, I did not enjoy that. It was a frightful thing. I knew I couldn't say anything about it and I was brainwashed that if I did, it was my fault and I was the bad girl. That's the only thing I remembered. By the same token, I had to tell my son about this situation. We cried and cried and cried, and he said "Mamma, the same person that did it to you introduced it to me." We talked about when it first happened and how it happened. After we finished talking, I got all my boys together to find out if they had been introduced to it. My second boy had been introduced to it, but he was more like me. He never approached my son Walter. I don't know why.

Ironically, this family member never approached my sister either, because we even talked about that. What I'm saying is, when he said that I would be considered a bad girl, yes and no, because my grandmother told me we must go to church on Sunday. I didn't know what salvation was at a very early age. All I knew is that I went to church. I had to go to church. I was told to go to church. So, it was like going to work. The only difference is I wasn't receiving a paycheck.

When I finally told my mother, she said, "But that's impossible." I said, "No mamma, not only did he do it to me, he did it to two of my sons. That's why I'm telling you." I said, "I did not go on the Oprah Show for show. I went on there to try to help people, to let them know that these things do exist in this world and you don't have to be quiet about a lot of things. I wanted to let people know these things don't have to be a stumbling block. You don't have to have low self-esteem, because things like this should make you want to grow, want to be somebody. That's why I did it."

When I was growing up, our family activities consisted of playing a lot of Chinese Checkers and Old Maids. On Saturday night, after we finished making gingerbread, you got a chance to either lick the bowl, or if there was enough there, you would put it in the oven and it was called a hoecake. We used to eat that and play Old Maids, Chinese Checkers or listen to the Barn Dance. There wasn't any television, so we used to sit around and listen to the radio, and this particular program came on the radio every Saturday night called the Barn Dance, which was square dancing. That was fun. I looked forward to that every Saturday.

I grew up in Chicago Heights, a small community where everybody knew everybody. The children that lived on the west side were the uppity, uppity. Those that went to Washington School looked on us as uppity, uppity. My grandfather owned a lot of property. My grandmother sang in the choir and my mother played the piano. We were considered middle class, but we were poor.

Everybody looked up to everybody, and that's the reason when my uncle molested me, you would have brought shame on the family being considered a bad girl, and no one would believe you. Since everybody knew everybody, you were very discreet about what you did. You didn't bring shame on the family at all.

When you started, as they say, "keeping company" with a little boy, it had to be someone with some status. You didn't go out with everybody. It had to be somebody that had something. Herman was my first boyfriend. His father was the iceman. Back then, we didn't have refrigerators, we had what you called an ice box. The iceman came down the street saying, "iceman, iceman" and you got the ice. I dated his son in high school. He was a football player, and a very mannerable young man, but they didn't know what their children were doing. Just because his father was the iceman, it didn't make him what he was. He was the first young man that got my cherry. It was more or less a play thing, but that was a secret that we kept and we were going to love each other until the day we died. We went our separate ways.

When I got pregnant before finishing high school, it was "You're getting married." You got married before you started showing. You brought no shame on the family. You get married to give the baby a name, love or no love. You didn't bring shame upon that baby, and all of this was done before you started showing. I couldn't finish high school, but those that were having sex but didn't get caught, went ahead and got their education, so you were now out of that class.

Ours was a close community. We had one Sunday School teacher, Charlotte Scott. The "good children" who lived on the west side all went to Sunday School. Their mothers had a part in the church. If you belonged to a certain church, you had status. The church my parents belonged to was the mother church of Chicago Heights, Union Baptist Church. I no longer belong there. If you did something wrong, they would give you a spanking.

Miss Charlotte Scott, for example, my Sunday School teacher at that time, if you did anything that was out of the ordinary and needed to be chastised, she would take a ruler or paddle and give you a spanking on your hand or fanny. Then she would tell your parents and you got another whipping.

Then there was the next-door neighbor. You never borrowed flour or sugar, because that was a sign you were in need. If you didn't have it, you went without. I remember when we started getting princess phones, those straight line phones, I think at that particular time, the monthly phone bill was like $4.13. My grandmother said, "We're going to use this phone economically." You never wanted the phone to get cut off, because the neighbors would find out that you really couldn't afford it. If any of this got out, it was a reflection you were poor. Well, we were poor. You didn't do things to let the community know you couldn't afford it or that you were poor. I think it was their pride and vanity.

In school, there were only two teachers I liked. That was when I was in Lincoln Grade School. They were Mrs. Genevieve Thompson, and I can't remember the one that used to teach us the hoola. They're both dead now. They motivated me a whole lot. I really didn't like when I had to move out of their class, because everything else became a bore to me. The one that taught the hoola, because I loved to dance, she kept me active. She used to have a lot of plays. I knew I was her pick, her favorite, so I got a chance to participate in all this and I loved it. Once I got out of her class, I went to another class before I went to Genevieve Thompson.

It was a bore and then Mrs. Genevieve Thompson was on the same order as the teacher that taught the hoola. I got motivated again. She told me some of the things my grandmother did about once you get it up here, in your head, no one can take it away. Learn a lot. She used to always say, "Your mom keeps you so clean. She dresses you so nice." That was another thing. We were identified by white teachers by the way we looked. They were both white teachers. My auntie was a beautician, so my hair was always in Shirley Temple curls. I always looked nice. There were certain ones that stood out among the white teachers and that was also status. If you weren't liked by them, you had a hard time. I knew I was their pick. I enjoyed being in their class. I enjoyed being in grade school, but I knew I had to go further. I hated Washington Junior High School.

In grade school, I got the attention I wanted and I knew I didn't have to deal with the uncle. Once I got home, I had to deal with him, because nine times out of ten, I wasn't going to my home, I was going to my mother's sister's home where the uncle was. I knew I could stay at school and do little odds and ends for my teachers, where I wouldn't have to run into that. Mind you, I couldn't say anything about this. When I got ready to go to Washington Junior High School, this is when the home parties started. Climbing out the window, the quarter parties and the whole bit. It seems like, whatever you're forbidden to do, you want to do it anyway. So, I went through that stage while in Washington Junior High School and high school.

When I got to Washington Junior High School, I got more involved with black teachers. Unlike the white teachers where you knew where they were coming from because you would be singled out, the black teachers put you in a group. Listen to what I'm saying. White teachers singled you out, so everybody in class knew you were their pet. If the black teachers liked you, they put you in a group. This group got in the Glee Club, but you knew how you got in the Glee Club. You were one of the black teacher's favorites. If the black teachers saw something in you, they would try their best to get you interested in it. Remember, I didn't like school when I was at Washington Junior High School. I don't know if it had anything to do with the uncle, but I rebelled against black teachers.

My grandfather was the only father image I had. Once I got married, he told me not to trust no man at all. I didn't know until later on, the reason he was telling me these things was because he was a devil himself. He was very whorish. He was an individual that not only went out on my grandmother, he also went out on the woman he was married to. So, he was teaching me the opposite, not to let a man come into my life and hurt me. He always thought people really didn't love each other. It was like who beat who in a relationship, and I learned from that.

He was very forceful. He had to be. He always told me, never let your guard down. Always be aware of what's around you. Listening from a man's point of view, I'm saying this to you, love and not love, and that stayed with me. It was, you don't love and let him not love. So, I was more or less taught by my uncle and my grandfather, "You don't get me, I get you." The name of the game was to be very forceful and not let the other person know you are like that. In other words, you run them over, not the other way around.

I had to be the leader. I always had to be the pushy one. I learned from that. It made me hard. I always had to achieve something. I never gave God credit for it. It wasn't until last year, when he showed me that. He said, "I'll give you anything you want, anything you ask me for. I've been good to you all this time, but you've got to acknowledge me sometimes. Put me first."

My husband and I did not stay in our relationship long. It was a ten-year relationship, and I don't believe I would have accomplished what I have today, if I had stayed in that marriage, because it was a bad marriage. My grandmother and my aunt helped me with my children. I lived up over my grandfather. All four boys were raised in that one house. We moved, after I separated from my husband. We moved into other living quarters, and every time I got ready to do something, I had to go to my grandmother. She would say to me, "You know, you really ought to get it together. Maybe you need to get married again." I knew that was not the answer.

I was instilling in my children that education was important to them. They were in grammar school and high school. I worked to see to it that they got as far as they could, but it wasn't until my son Walter got his college degree that the light bulb lit up. I said to myself, he's going to be making X amount of money, and I was determined that I wouldn't let my children outdo me. This is what I had instilled in them. I thought, How come I can't do that? So, I started back to school. I went back and got my high school diploma and went to college and then got a trade. I began to be somebody.

When I was in seventh or eight grade, I didn't like school, but I love it now. Number one, I have to pay for all this knowledge myself. When you're under mom and dad's roof, they're paying for it and the old saying is, you appreciate things once you have to scuffle and pay it out of your pocket. That old saying is true, because you don't want to see your money go to waste. When you become an adult, time is money and it plays a great role in your life. You're not going to waste that precious time. Time is money and the same with schooling; so you learn to appreciate schooling when you get older.

I went to Thornton Community College, with the help of Bloom High School. I always wanted my high school diploma. I did not want a GED because to me a GED, even though that exam is not that easy, wouldn't satisfy me. There was something about getting the high school diploma. I had made up my mind, I'm going back to get my high school diploma, and I did at age forty. After getting my high school diploma, I said, I'm not working for nobody, no more. I'm going back and get a trade. So, I took those college credits and turned them into taking up a trade. I went to a Mortuary College of Science. Dr. Connie Long was the one that motivated me to go to mortuary school. I just admired Connie. I admired her when she got married, and when she got divorced. She had two children to take care of and her parents and that in itself motivated me. When she came back to Chicago Heights, we talked and I just knew I wanted better out of life. She motivated me in that way, even though we sometimes get into the biggest arguments. I still didn't like working, punching a clock for somebody else. I wanted something of my own. I eventually went back and took other classes to learn different things. I am a freelancer.

It wasn't until this situation with my son, and God spoke to me and said, "If you abide in me, I will abide in you and all things will be given unto you. But, you've got to obey me and do my will." I'm a hat lover. People always say to me, "I'm going to take that hat off your head", or "Can I have that?" and the light bulb lit up. I said, why don't you sell them, instead of letting people take them off your head and saying they always want them? So, I got established. I got the business telephone guide and got different wholesale companies and started sending my applications out and became one of their distributors. So, I sell hats.

When I went out and attempted to do what I'm doing now, I had no idea how I was going to do it, where the money was going to come from. There were weeks when I didn't make any money, but my bills got paid every week. Every month, my bills got paid and it was just on faith.

One of the greatest obstacles I've had to deal with in my life was being a single parent, because I was not at home. There were times when I had to raise my children over the phone. I can remember working two jobs for them to have the same type of education they had before their father and I divorced. I wanted them to go to a parochial school. I had to take two jobs to do it. My income did not warrant some of things they had when their father and I were together, so that was a struggle. I had to get my grandmother involved where she would be there to watch my children. There were times when she stayed at my house weeks and weeks, and I couldn't even afford to pay her.

My children didn't do without the necessities, because I was smart enough to know how to manage. They didn't know a lot of things. One of my jobs was working for a realtor and contractor. I became his lover. There were a lot of things my children didn't know. I remember the first charge card I got, he was the co-signer. A mother should not have to go through that, especially having boys.

The reason I made it was nothing but determination. I knew what I didn't want. I knew that. I knew a long time ago, when I worked for those Jewish people, I did not want to work for nobody. I did not want to have no one telling me what to do. There were certain things that I heard, and I didn't want no one telling me that, because it made me feel like a slave, and I don't even know what slavery was like. I wasn't back there then, but I could just imagine and I said, well, how am I going to deal with this. I said, do it.

I think other people don't overcome obstacles because of low self-esteem and dwelling on the problem at hand. Remember what happened to my son and what happened to me? The same family member introduced that situation to us. It made him resort to homosexuality. It made me resort to being forceful, wanting to be more than what I was and to let the black man know, that you're not going to step on me. You're not going to beat me and abuse me sexually and physically.

I believe welfare has made a lot of men lazy, and with the women not being educated, succumb to the flesh, the natural self wants a man, because first of all they have low self-esteem, no job, no ambition, no nothing; so they have more babies. Men must know they have to work and we're no longer going to take care of their children. They've got to learn some kind of responsibility. To do that, you've got to give that person a job. I think some people get into a rut. I think in a lot of situations, people are buried alive. They have nobody to motivate them and especially with today's economy.

To get yourself out of the rut, you have to be around people who are going places, who are motivated, who are doing things and got money in their pocket. When they want to go buy a steak dinner, they've got some money to go buy it. They don't have to break in your house or my house to get what they want. They've got to be around people that's going to give them that motivation. The only way you're going to learn is by listening to people talk, being around people who are doing something and having that ambition to want to do something.

I believe people are in the wrong places. They're among the wrong peers. They don't go to any seminars or any motivational meetings. I'm nosy, I've always had nose trouble. I've got all sorts of books in my home. I just picked up an African wedding book that dates all the way back to our ancestors, and I'm going to take that and utilize it. I'm going to specialize in African weddings, but I've got to educate my people first. We've still got people that can't relate to being black. A lot of things were stripped from us. We do have a culture.

I can't remember if it was Martin Luther King or who that said, "A mind is a terrible thing to waste." I believed that. I believe we don't use one-fourth of our minds, and whatever you set your mind to, you can be successful in it.

To be successful takes knowing more than one thing. Being black, I think most white people who are successful are so, because they have a tendency to fall into it, because someone in the family has set the way for them. But, if you don't have that, you've got to make up in your mind this is what I want to be, this is what I want to do, and you go for it. I really do believe that you can make any amount of money you want. We're going to fall into a lot of obstacles, because we are black and there's a lot of racism in this country, a lot of prejudice, but I know a lot of black people that are successful. It's what you have made up here in your head. Like my grandmother said, "Once you get it up here, can't nobody take that away from you."

As an adult, I was doing a lot of things that were not Christ-like. God gave me a lot of talent. I have a way of influencing people to my way of thinking; I'm not bragging. That can be good or bad, but I do know I have a way about me that people will follow me. I have a way about creating different things, putting different things together, putting a program together. It doesn't take me six months or a year. I can put a program together in a month and raise $10,000. I believe that's a gift. So, the ministry and the congregation saw that.

Most Baptist people concentrate on the almighty dollar and to see how many programs they can get together. All I knew is, I would be contacted on the phone, "We've got to have this done." Yet and still, I was committing every sin there was, and getting up making announcements, and one time I was the assistant superintendent of the primary department. I wasn't worthy of it. There were times, I can remember a minister would come from out of town and you made him "happy" when he came to town. It was one of those ordeals. Believe me, it's nothing to be proud of. It's nothing to brag or boast about. I'm just saying what does go on, and we say we're Christians. We go to church every Sunday and prayer meeting every Wednesday.

I believe where there's no restriction, there's no conviction. When there's no sin brought to you over the pulpit, you feel as though you can do anything you want to do. How can you have any convictions? I wasn't convicted going to bed with the deacon, going to bed with the trustee and then heading up programs.

But certain things hit you. No one would have ever made me believe that my son could have turned that way. You're not born that way. I tried everything in my power to make him understand that. He was saved at the church I belong to now; so he knows a little bit about salvation. He just got turned around. When God speaks to us, and we don't hearken to his call, he'll turn you over to a reprobate mind. Believe me, after all of this happened, God dealt with me for one year and he said, "You're spiritually dead.   You're doing everything under the sun. You're going to hell. Everybody that says Lord, Lord is not going to enter into the kingdom." These were the things he was talking to me about, and they were piercing things. When I would hear certain messages over the radio, the truth was hitting me. God really didn't start blessing me, until I stopped sinning.

That's how I'm growing in my religion now. There are some things that I don't understand about the Bible. I'm in a very militant church, and there are some things I don't understand why we have to do them, but like I said before, where there's no restrictions, there's no convictions.

8

Refuge from the Storm: Edward's Story

Edward is a forty-six-year-old college-educated African-American male. He has lived most of his life in an all black community and is a community activist. Edward projects a sense of altruism and confidence that betrays a childhood torn by alcoholism and abuse. Through a community organization, he finds a surrogate father who brings order and stability to his life.

My mother went as far as the eighth grade. My father got to the third grade in school. They were both born in the South. My father served in World War II. He was a part of the force that invaded Normandy with the Allied Forces. In 1945, he was honorably discharged and he and my mother got married. The racial situation there was not good in the South. Having fought in World War II, father returned to the South where he was still treated with racial indecencies and indignations by whites.

He vividly remembered getting upset for getting thrown out or disrespected in a restaurant or tavern. It was so bad he ended up turning over a white man's car. He literally turned it over and burned it, and they chased after him. He was engaged to my mother at that time. So, I understand they got married the following week or two, real quick, because they had to get out of town. They had to get out of the State. They got money from his mother to escape and come to Chicago because the white klansmen were out to kill him. An older sister who was living in Chicago made arrangements for him and his new bride.

They lived with my father's oldest sister, Bertha, on the southside of Chicago. It was in an apartment building and that apartment building was where I was born. We moved in 1949 to Edgewater. Mother had a cousin there. My family couldn't adjust very well to city life, because they were farmers. My mother's cousin rented my parents one of his apartments in Edgewater. They saw Edgewater was still a rural setting, very similar to the way the South was where they'd come from. We lived there for about two or three years, then we moved just across the alley into a house. In December of 1954, we moved into the newly opened projects in Edgewater.

I was told we were the second family to move into the projects. I know it was pretty empty when we moved there. We lived there for nine years.

Edgewater was a community that some historians like to say was a planned community. I disagree with that to some extent. But a lot of things happened indirectly and I don't think it was planned to be a black community. It just turned out that way. Edgewater actually began as a community of interracial families. The town was named after a father and son named Edgewaters. They were white, and they were real estate investors and speculators who subdivided the area just after the turn of the century, but they couldn't sell the land. They thought the city was expanding and thought it was going to eventually gobble up this section of Edgewater and they would make a lot of money. This didn't happen and they began to sell the land for very little money.

They knew of some interracial families in the city who were not adjusting very well to the white community or the black community. They weren't accepted in either one, believe it or not. They were mulattos, and they were invited to come out and look at the land out here and start their own little settlement. The land was so very cheap, it was very attractive for them to come here and they did. They got along well and it became a haven for interracial couples and families. That's how it really began. It was attractive for blacks, in general, not just the mulattos. And that's how the town began to develop also.

The mixture between white and black I guess makes a nice mix. The women here were extremely attractive to the point white men from Bridgeton frequented here quite a bit and would solicit these very attractive mulatto women. And a lot of problems resulted from that, including the development of a prostitution house, literally. There were several, and one did quite well. This is where the white men would come. As a result of that, some children were born and they were clearly mulatto, and that became a problem.

There was no police department to keep the peace or discipline them. So it was suggested by Bridgeton officials to Edgewater residents at the time that they get their own police department. So, Thomas Turner, Richard Bloom and Leroy Keller said, maybe this is what we should do. They wanted to find a way to protect their women because their women were being harassed at bus stops, train stations by these white men and that was really the bottom line.

As I grew up in Edgewater, we had outdoor toilets. Although we had a bathroom with a bathtub and toilet in it, we never used it because the village didn't have a sewer system at that time to connect it to. What was the point of having it? I guess, we were hoping it was coming soon. But we continued to use the outhouse and slop jars too. We bathed in tin tubs up against the heater, taking a bath one at a time in the same bath water. It was hard.

I remember the floods we used to have in Edgewater. We had to get in boats and row to the store and get bread. And I remember the outbreak of the epidemic we had when a bacteria disease broke out in the village, because of the poor sanitation system. We all had to be vaccinated over and over again. I remember the shots. That was later corrected and we did all right, but employment was still very low. We didn't have much, but we felt like we did. Greens, chitterlings, pork chops and chicken, that was the order of the day.

As I remember, most of the people worked in either the steel mills, stock yards, the nearby Libby factory or for the railroad. Outside that, people were allowed to have livestock, which many of them did, and they had gardens and raised their food, for the most part. There were women working as domestic helpers for whites.

In those days, you could still go away and leave your house unlocked and come back. There was no problem with people breaking in houses. That just didn't happen. People helped each other. There was still discipline and respect. When one family would discipline another child from another family, if they saw them doing something wrong, nothing would be said about it other than you did wrong and you might get another whipping from your parents when it was told what you did.

We were very neighborly. We played together and we made things together like sling shots. We used to make little toy boats and stuff. We used to go hiking through the woods, picking the apples off the trees and climbing the canal bank. I thought childhood was great. People were much more neighborly, much more so than they are to-day.

I think things started to change with the Civil Rights movement and the breakdown of morals across this country, with the drug culture coming in and the hippie movement. All that had some effect, I think, but it was not that great in Edgewater because the national change had only ripple effects on little towns like Edgewater. Certainly, at the school level, we were dressing in whatever the style was. If it was the hippie, we would dress hippie style. Of course, I personally didn't. I was very conservative.

I think people thought because I was quiet I was smart in school. I was, academically, a lower than average student in terms of academic grades. My grades averaged between C and D. But people think when you're quiet, you're smart but that was not my case. Then I found out later, it wasn't that I was dumb, I just never studied. I was never really motivated to study. My parents only were concerned that we got up every morning and went to school and came home. They did not help us with our homework, because they couldn't. Their poor educational background did not allow them and they were embarrassed to try to help us with our homework, because they just couldn't.

I liked school. One unfortunate thing happened to me in the fourth grade, I think it was. I actually flunked (failed) in fourth grade. Ms. Davidson was the teacher that flunked me. That was her first year teaching job and I guess she was out to prove to the world that she was going to be the master teacher and that she could not only pass students, but she could also flunk them, if they didn't do what they were supposed to do. Maybe I deserved it. I didn't think so.

This was one of the things I prided my godfather for. He was very upset when he heard I had failed that year and he wanted an explanation from the principal and the teacher. He tried to get my parents involved but they just said, "If you can get it done, well fine, if not then he may have to repeat." But he insisted. He asked them to compare my grades with those of students who passed and found a serious discrepancy. My grades were just as good as some of those who passed. And between him and the principal, they made a decision that they were going to get me in my right grade. They were going to make the adjustment but somehow, I don't know why, it never happened. I was transferred on to Douglass School and the paper got fouled up. He even tried then to get it straightened out and it just never occurred.

I was always that one year behind. But I'm kind of glad it happened, because I liked the class I graduated with. There were classmates who had an effect on me. I remember Geraldine and Wilma, because they were the two smartest ones in class and I always wanted to be with the smart kids. But I wasn't smart, so I couldn't compete. They would be on the honor roll and I wouldn't. That was something I always wanted. But they motivated me to try harder, because I knew they studied hard. And I said, "Well, I just don't want to study." And I didn't. I don't remember seriously studying at all, and that's what made me think when I got in high school, I said, "My God, I've got the same diploma and I graduated the same day with all these other people and their diploma was no different than mine and yet they are honor students." I said, "Well, gee whiz, if I can get the same paper and didn't study, what would have happened if I had studied?" I thought about that and that's what motivated me through college.

But when I was in junior high school, my mind goes back that there were two male friends that had a great influence on me and that's because they were smart. Two guys, Bob Madison and Theodore Adams. They were "A" students and they were males I could relate to. And I wanted to be with that group of smart guys. They were kind of trying to keep me out, because I wasn't as smart as they were. I couldn't compete with them. And then Anthony came in and he was more my level. So, both of us would try to compete to be with the clique of Theodore Adams and Bob Madison, because they were "A" students, and finally we were accepted into their little clan. So, they were inspirational. It was a positive role that they played and for the first time, Anthony and I studied.

I always looked for the better things in life somehow. Some natural instinct I think that's just innate. I can't think of anything in particular that motivated me other than I've always had a desire to be better or to do better. I think it was from my involvement in the Edgewater Boys Club by Rev. Johnson, because that was all he ever taught. He taught that you could be better, that you could do better and you can be the best and you can achieve whatever you want if you have the will and desire to do so. But it takes hard work. And I know he always preached to us "never be afraid of hard work."

All of my teachers through elementary school and junior high were black, as I recall. I did not experience white teachers until my junior year in high school. There is one black English teacher that stands out in my mind a lot, Mrs. McDonald. Mrs. McDonald was a superior teacher. She was a more learned and prepared teacher. She knew how to teach to the point where you could learn. If you made a mistake, she had a way of correcting you without embarrassing you, and if you did something well, she made sure she rewarded you with applauds. She'd say in class, "Clap for Edward." She would play games with us and that made learning interesting.

I recall learning the Roman numerals under her, that was really interesting to me. She would go down the line and ask everybody to say the Roman numerals. If you didn't say it correctly, she would stop you, before she went to the next person. Everybody was hung up on the number six. Nobody could get past six in roman numerals, until she got to me. When she got to me, I said, "VI" and she said, "correct." Everybody looked, "What did he do?" and I went on and finished it. It was little things like that which also encouraged me.

I also remember another black teacher, Mrs. Smith, because as a kid I suffered from a heart ailment. Now that I am an adult, I've discovered that I also have a hearing impairment. The heart ailment was discovered early in my childhood, but the hearing impairment never came out. I now believe that was part of the reason I didn't learn well. I wasn't hearing very well. I thought I was hearing, but as a child, you don't know you're not hearing if you can hear in one ear. You don't know you're supposed to hear in both ears. I was never hearing in my left ear.

I would always sit in the middle or toward the back of the class, because I was always afraid to sit in the front. I didn't have the nerve. I thought the front was really for the smart kids. If you sit in the front, you get singled out. I was afraid of being singled out with, Edward tell us this or tell us that or would you read this, or would you go to the blackboard. If you're in the back, your chances of being called on is less.

My heart problem was really bad between the sixth grade and eight grade. I recall an incident where I had an attack in the auditorium. Everybody was upset, and they rushed me to the hospital. When I returned to school, I was given the royal treatment. Mrs. Smith did not allow anybody to walk in the center of the room. She had these chairs arranged in a strange fashion around the room, and did not allow anyone to walk in the center of the room. When you left the classroom, you had to put your chair on top of the desk. Her room was immaculately clean all the time, especially the center of the room.

The teachers and kids sent me cards and money. They took up a collection for me. I was in the hospital for quite a while. When I returned to school, everything was so gentle, Edward had to be handled gently. They would have to put my chair up for me. I was not allowed to put my chair up. Everything was done for me, "No, you don't have to walk around the room Edward. You come right across the front, right across the center." So maybe, I made history that time, because she didn't allow anyone to walk in the center of her room. That was death. She would not allow me to lift anything heavy or strenuous, or that she felt would effect my heart. She was afraid to do that. I made the honor roll that year.

I will never forget, a minister, Rev. Hinton, was brought out to pray for me the week before I was scheduled to have the operation. Believe it or not, when I went back to the doctors, they said the hole in my heart had disappeared, and I never had the surgery.

My mother did different kinds of work. I don't recall her doing domestic work for hire, but she used to go to the field when the old Libby factory was there in Bridgeton and pick tomatos, she and some of her girlfriends that lived in Edgewater. She was the sole supporter and provider for our family, taking odd jobs here and there. She worked for the Edgewater Cab Company for a number of years. When the Edgewater Cab Company first opened under Mr. Jimmy Morgan, she was his first operator there for many years. She worked in various taverns in Edgewater as a barmaid. Then in 1968, she went to work for a hospital.

My father did construction work at the time. He was called a general laborer. It was seasonal work, so he would only work during the warmer months, and then of course, in the winter months he was just unemployed and lived off his unemployment. He developed a real serious drinking problem which disabled him from holding a meaningful job. My mother always worked. I even recall her working for the Edgewater, Public Works Department. In those day, they cleaned out septic tanks by hand with a bucket and my mother was one of the few females that did that work to provide for her family.

As early as I can remember, my father had a drinking problem. This goes back to when I was at least six years old. My mother told me he actually started drinking as a child. As a teenager, he always had a drinking problem, but it didn't become really severe until about 1952, when he started drinking excessively, and it just continued until today, even. My father constantly drank. Constantly there were fights in the house in front of us and with his friends, with other women that would be there and relatives that would be there. They'd drink and fight and this was disturbing to me as a child. It had an effect on me because everytime a fight would break out, I would get so weak. I would fall to the floor many times and would have to crawl to my bedroom, because it upset me so bad. I would cry a lot, watching these fights. It was something I just deplored. It did have an effect on me, especially when I saw my father fight my uncles. They'd tear down the doors and tear up furniture, and my mother would just be stressed when she'd come home from work to see all this.

Now, he has developed cancer and all kinds of medical problems. It's amazing. He's now seventy-one years old, still drinks; has had multiple operations, lung removed, liver problems and has cancer spreading all over his body, and amazingly, he's still drinking. Both of my parents are still living. Amazingly, they have never been separated, except when he goes on his drinking binges, she may have to run away for a day or two at my house, if he started jumping the family, and he has done this several times.

There have been some violence in the family, but not only against my mother, but against my sister and even my brother, as a result of his drinking problem. He is also illiterate in that he can't read or write even today. He can sign his name, but that's it. He doesn't do to badly with numbers, now. He can count money very well. He can add and subtract pretty good, but that's about the extent of what he knows. He's very content with where he is now, even though he's becoming more of a problem as he get older. He retired very early. Maybe retirement is the wrong word. He quit work. He quit work almost thirty years ago. He was in his late thirties when he stopped working, period, due to alcoholism.

My parents had good moral backgrounds in terms of knowing right from wrong and teaching us the good things as opposed to the bad things. They taught us values. Drinking is something my mother deplored, and then we saw the problem with that with my father. Respecting elders was a prime concern. When we did something wrong or bad, we got whipped. My mother or father would do that. I think my father took a lot of his anger out on us, when he whipped us, because we weren't whipped with switches. My mother whipped us with a switch. But my father would whip us with an extension cord, something that had some wire in it. It only took one or two whippings like that for me and I tell you, he had no more problems out of me. I would run under the bed and my hair was long at that time, and would get tangled up under the springs of the bed when I ran from him and he'd catch me that way. Because my brother's complexion was very fair like my mother's, whippings like the ones we got from our father would be visible on his body for days and looked horrible. I had the same amount of whip marks on my body, but because my complexion is dark, the marks were not so visible. My sister was not disciplined as severely as we were, because she was more self-disciplined and a female. He didn't have much problems with her at all.

I used to hear my mother say, she was very proud of the way she raised her children, as opposed to the way she sees children raised today. She says as she recalls, she looks at the problems parents are having with their children and she'd say, "I didn't have this kind of problem with my children." She often talks about how glad she was that we never got in any serious trouble while we were in our teenage years. I think this was because when we were kids, we always had something to do. We'd shoot marbles or play ball and jacks or my sister would jump rope or we'd play games like hide and seek or red light, green light. These were things you don't see today. We were involved in the Boys Club with activities, especially me and my brother. My brother got very interested in football. Football was a very strong point for him.

At that time, I thought the discipline was hard. Now that I look back upon it, I think it was proper and correct except for the discipline my father gave. When he would punish us it was always violent, in my opinion, because he would hit us with his fists from time to time. Most of the time, it was done when he was drinking. He was drunk when he whipped us and that was what really got me.

What really hurt me too was the time my father was shot with a gun. He doesn't talk a lot about it. He doesn't want to talk about it. I've been trying to get it out of him, but I got some information lately on some things that happened. He was shot while we were children living in Edgewater, and he actually died on the operating table at the hospital. They were able to resuscitate him. He was shot at least four or five times through the torso part of his body. Bullets are still in his spine today that can't be removed.

It happened because of some things he was involved in at the time involving gangster activity, people dealing in drugs and bootlegging and that kind of stuff. I remember him coming in the back door. I probably wasn't more than eight years old. I remember this vividly. He just slumped over the chair. Blood was running everywhere and my sister was screaming to the top of her voice. My mother and my cousin across the way got him to the hospital, and fortunately he survived. It could have been very, very tragic for him, but he always seemed to have been in that negative element.

My relationship with my brother and sister was very good overall, but it was a very different kind of relationship. I really think this happened early in our lives. In fact, I can almost tell you the exact year it happened. I was nine years old.

In the earlier days in the 50s and the very early 60s, not past '62 or '63, there were clubs. There were Boys Clubs, Girls Clubs and a lot of church organizations that had youth programs that kept youngsters involved with activities that kept them out of trouble. There was a club in Edgewater called the Edgewater Boys Achievement Club. This was like a boys' club and Rev. Johnson was the founder of this organization along with Mrs. Hopson and a number of other people who I can't remember now. Mr. Chappel and some others that lived in Edgewater, started this organization just to keep boys off the street and doing things constructive to keep them out of trouble, basically. It was very nice.

My brother had joined the club and he would come home with so many exciting things. I liked it. There were crafts which they would make wallets, belts and play games and go on trips. So, I got excited and I wanted to join, but I was too young. You had to be ten years old. But they saw how enthusiastic I was about it and allowed me to come in at age nine. We participated in all the parades and we wore military uniforms.

But Rev. Johnson was a minister. He added a very strong religious connotation to the club and we would sing gospel songs and visit churches, hospitals and other organizations and sing gospel. I had taken a real strong liking to music at this time and it was noticeable to everybody that I liked music, singing and playing the piano, even though I couldn't play. So, Rev. Johnson noticed this and encouraged me to pursue this part of my desires and I did. He helped me get involved in taking piano lessons from Mrs. Olgsby. She was my music teacher and that's where I learned to play.

Then, Rev. Johnson formed his own church outside of the Edgewater Boys Club, and I became a strong member in the church. I was in the Sunday School. All of these activities were leading me toward greater involvement in the church, but my brother did not follow. My brother stayed in the club, but he did not go the route I went, the church part. He was more the type that wanted to stay out in the streets. But I stayed in the church and there was starting to develop the difference between my brother, my sister and me.

My sister wasn't fortunate to become a part of any kind of social club like a Girls' Club. We didn't have them at that time. There was the one club for the boys and there was a club for the girls, I think it was the majorettes. But my sister was not interested in anything like that. She loved children. She was always babysitting or taking care of somebody's kids. That was her thing and it is today too. So, she stayed at home pretty much. That's the way our lives sort of developed, together and yet separate. Even though we were raised together, we pursued very different occupations and social interests. My interest in the church became very, very strong and very involved. I became a Sunday school teacher, later a Sunday school superintendent, and the next thing I knew I was a church musician. I remember one day, I had to play the piano, had to teach Sunday school and then had to preach, all that happened one Sunday. The pastor didn't show up and the word was sent to me to preach and there I was.

Rev. Johnson was also a businessman. He had a store. He was a well-educated man. He had a bachelor's degree and a very strong interest in education. He passed that on to us in the Boys' Club, to get an education, to be somebody important. He instilled some very strong values in all of us, and I would say more than half of the boys in that club were very successful later in life.

I really give a lot of credit to my godfather, Rev. Johnson, for instilling in me the kind of fatherly love and support I needed, and I wish my brother and sister had had also. I had a very good relationship with Rev. Johnson, one I would say was responsible for bringing out in me what I think was already in me more so. It probably wouldn't have been had he not been there. One of the things I liked was he actually started teaching his own children six girls and one boy or had us teaching them how to read the Bible and write before they were in school. They, literally, learned their alphabets and word structure and everything by reading the Bible and you know how hard the Bible is to read. As it turned out, it worked to their advantage because they were all superior in school and successful in life.

Then he opened a business and I worked in his store, starting at age thirteen, as a stock boy. The store was in Edgewater. He had three stores, all totaled. When he closed one, he'd build a larger one, occupy a larger one. When I got to be about sixteen or seventeen, he made me co-owner of the store. I was really excited then. I had my name as co-owner, on business cards, gee whiz! We had great plans of expanding the store into a mini-mall, that was what the plan was going to be. We were going to have a laundromat in there. We were going to attach some other stores to it that would be a mini-mall concept. That was the idea. But, as I got older and towards the end of high school and getting ready for college, I was having different thoughts about business. I didn't like business. I really didn't. I did it because it was a job and I could make some money and it kept money in my pockets. But, I didn't like the long hours. I would have to work there longer than other people that worked there, being co-owner and all. I think that's what discouraged me about business. The accounting and all of that, the paperwork was just something I didn't want to deal with. But anyway, it taught me some valuable things about how business operates. I learned how to deal with people.

Then came pressure about going to college. He was prepared to finance my college education, but I was starting to feel guilty about some of the things I had as opposed to what my brother and sister had and my friends too. I thought, I'm getting quite a bit here and nobody else seems to. So, I decided I wasn't going to let him send me to college. I was going to do that on my own.

Another businessman, Mr. Kelly, didn't take an interest in me but his wife. They owned Kelly's Store. He had a program where he was going to help finance or provide some scholarship money to worthy youngsters in Edgewater to go to college. I was not his pick. I guess he said Rev. Johnson could take care of me. He was going to take care of Andrew Smith and Ralph Cook and Floyd Young, those three. But, his wife wanted me. She wanted to help me. So, it was decided he would help support my college education, mainly because of his wife pursuing it.

It turned out that I turned them both down. Again, I felt the obligation factor. I didn't want to be obligated to anybody in case I failed, because when I started writing to these colleges, they were all turning me down. They were telling me my grade point average wasn't high enough to get in college. I thought you could just go to college. I didn't know you had to meet requirements. Nobody ever told me you've got to study in high school and do well.

I remember a counselor in high school telling me I shouldn't go to college. He said because my aptitude and family background was such that I should devote more time to vocational skills and don't consider college at all. He was white. So, I didn't know the difference.

I always wanted to play tennis. In high school they told me in my sophomore year I couldn't play tennis until I got into my junior year, which is the varsity level. But when I got to varsity and stopped in, they said you've got to have some background, you should have had some experience. I didn't realize I was being discriminated against at the time, but I was. I could of been maybe an Arthur Ashe by now. But I never got the opportunity because it was denied me. I didn't even know I was being discriminated against, but it was there. It was happening all around me and I had no knowledge until later.

Anyway, the fact they told me I shouldn't go to college and this and that, I decided that it would be my challenge to go to college. In other words, to do something that they said I couldn't do. I just determined on my own I was going to find a way to go to college. All the schools turned me down. I even applied to Harvard. Everybody sent me letters saying no, your high school transcripts are too poor, no way. So, I pleaded with Dr. Dulger the Dean at the college. I'll never forget him. He was the Dean of the school. He listened to me. I came in his office and he set me down and he said, "Well, what makes you think you can do it?" and I said, "Well, I want to go to college. I always thought I would but everybody's turned me down and I know I can do the work." He said, "You sound like a very determined person. If you can keep that determination, you can make it." But he said, "What we are going to do, I'll do this for you, I'll let you in on a probationary basis and if you do well the first semester, then we will put you on full status." And I said, "OK, give me that chance."

I didn't even know how to pick courses at that time. Do you know my first semester, I picked eighteen semester hours and maintained a B+ average and made the Dean's List. He was so proud of me. Even when I graduated, I was surprised that most of the people from high school that attended with me didn't even finish. They didn't make it, but I did. When I left there, I got a job working for a company. I was a summer student and ended up staying on full time. That was what paid for the rest of my college education.

The first goal in my life was to get a college education. That was a big test for me. It was something I had determined early in life I was going to do, no matter what. I had set some goals for myself. I always wanted to own my own home, a car, have a diploma on the wall, a degree, travel and write a book. Those were my goals, nothing beyond that.

I have accomplished all of those goals, except the completion of my book, and I feel very comfortable, very satisfied now. To me, success means wanting to accomplish something, doing what it takes to get it and accomplishing it. That's what I did. I knew I had to work hard to get what I wanted and it happened. I'm very pleased and satisfied with my life.

It wasn't my intention to remain in the village where I grew up. I had planned to leave. I had no idea that I was going to remain here. I thought I would move on some place else. I think one of the biggest things was the fact my family was still here, and I wanted to be close to my family. In the process, I got real caught up in the history of Edgewater. I saw the few people that had an appreciation for history were fading out, and nobody was going to carry this on. I felt a strong obligation to try to do something to salvage this history, because Edgewater has one of the most exciting histories of any community, I think, in the United States, to be so small. There's an immense amount of history here that needs to be recorded, documented and publicly displayed. That was a motivating factor; maybe I can serve in this capacity.

At the time, our town was steadily going down economically. It was not developing. It was still in poverty, and I said, "Maybe I can contribute something. Somebody invited me to a political meeting. I went and raised a lot of questions. I wanted to know why the village officials weren't doing certain things. What were they doing with the money, what's happening to improvement, what's happening to housing development, and parks. I began to see all these problems and somebody said, If you can see all of this, why don't you get involved yourself?"

I was insulted by the way it was said to me. So, I said, "I just might do that." I hadn't the faintest idea of how to get involved or get on the ballot. I talked to some people about it and they told me how. I began to do a lot of reading on election laws. I said, OK, I think I can do it. So, I got involved. I started as a precinct captain, to get my feet wet. They finally slated me at a convention to run for another office. From that point on, I began to know all there is to know, and now that I understand it thoroughly, I'm here.

I succeeded because I stayed in the black community. If I tried to do this in a white community, the outcome might be different. The competitiveness, definitely, would have been different. I knew I could do well here, because I felt that I was very popular here, because of my involvement with the church here as a musician, businessman and church leader. I have probably played the piano for every major church in Edgewater, and a lot of the small ones. People watched me, they knew me, knew my background. If I couldn't make it here, I couldn't make it anywhere. So, when election time came, I was a shoo-in. I was the top vote-getter.

I believe racism is the bottom line why black males are experiencing such difficulty in our society. Black males are still discriminated against, no matter how educated they are. We still have to work twice as hard, have two or three more degrees than the others. I think black males are suffering because of the male ego. The black male ego is threatening to the white male, in terms of masculinity. A black male is considered a sex object. We can't ignore that. It's becoming more apparent now than ever. White men feel threatened. They've always felt threatened by the black male, especially an educated black male.

Charles Evers, my seventh grade social studies teacher at Douglass School, very clearly pointed this out. His brother was Medgar Evers, the slain civil rights activist. Mr. Evers would frequently deviate from teaching the normal subject to tell us black students about the problems that exist in the South and throughout the United States between blacks and whites. He talked about the segregation problem, how he and his brother suffered a lot of indignities, as black youngsters.

He recalled an incident where there was a Ku Klux Klan gathering, and they saw these men with the sheets on. They were talking against blacks. One of the klansmen pointed at him and his little brother standing by looking on and said, "If you're not careful, them two little niggers there will one day be over you, if we don't keep them in their place." In other words, if we let them learn to read and write, they will conquer us. He said he never forgot that, and it was his desire to do just that, especially when his father owned a funeral home and they bombed it. He was a business man, and they thought no nigger should be in business. They are not smart enough to do that, and they shouldn't be allowed to anyway. The underlying message here was, whites have always known that blacks are just as capable of learning as they are. We have the same ability to do whatever whites can do, and even better. That's certainly been proven. I don't know why we had to prove it to begin with. That was something I remember.

I pat myself on the back. I have lived a pretty decent, honest life in front of people and my family. I'm very comfortable with that. I don't worry about who I wronged, because I haven't wronged anybody. I don't owe anybody anything. There are far more people that owe me, and I don't expect to get it back. If I can help, I do it because it's the humane thing to do.

Part II

RECURRING THEMES

9

On Solid Ground I Stand: Family Roots

At the most fundamental level, family (consanguine or surrogate) tended to shape the destiny of the storytellers. It was the foundation upon which all they were or hoped to become was built. Their oral histories resonated with clarity the significant role of the family in their lives. It was their experiences within the family that gave definition to self and chartered their course for the future.

While their family structures and dynamics played like a symphony with its many different parts, each was woven together by the repetition of a common theme. Characteristic of each family was a strong work ethic, parental supervision, values clarification, strict discipline, positive parental or significant-other role models and an underlying message of hope.

FAMILY VALUE SYSTEM

The family value system, beliefs, and attitudes figured prominently as factors in the more positive direction the storytellers lives ultimately took. Most studies on achievement of children from poor families have been myopic, focusing on either the composition of the household, especially the absence of the father, or other patterns of interaction that take place within the family related to the income and educational level of the parents. They fail to recognize that it is the more pervasive quality of the family's lifestyle, not the composition or socioeconomic status, that is the determining factor in the academic success of black children (Clark, 1983).

They also fail to acknowledge the positive and decisive impact on school success the manner in which parents think and behave as well as the interpersonal relationship they have with their children. Clark further contends that "children receive essential 'survival knowledge' for competent classroom role enactment from their exposure to positive home attitudes and encounters" (p.1). It is, therefore, important to identify how this knowledge is organized and transmitted to children within the home environment.

Clark found that the success with which families transmit survival skills and success knowledge is a complexed phenomenon that reaches back in time to the child-rearing practices of the previous generation and extends to include such variables as the parents' degree of social integration into the community, self-esteem, level of satisfaction with the home environment, social relationships, and support networks. He concluded that it is the family's beliefs, activities, and general cultural style that form the basic mindset for academic success.

He also observed essential variations in patterns of interaction between parents and children who developed social competencies and those who did not. He identified two communication styles parents used to prepare their children for major roles in life—sponsored independence and unsponsored independence. Sponsored independence was conducive to social competence. Parents who displayed this pattern of interaction were actively involved in their children's lives, expressing an open interest in all of their activities. They monitored the children's use of time and space and established a pattern of parent/child interaction that became the vortex for such activities as studying, reading, and writing. Furthermore, these parents provided their children with feedback in the form of explanations and advisement. They served as role models by the consistent demonstration of life skills and set standards for expected behavior. They provided positive reinforcement in the form of praise.

Conversely, homes characterized by unsponsored independence were not conducive to social competence. Parenting in these homes was characterized as authoritarian and permissive. There was limited parental interest and involvement in the children's activities inside and outside the home; infrequent shared activities such as reading, writing, teaching, advising, demonstrating ideas and concepts; standards for responsible behavior were either inconsistent or nonexistent; and parental behavior was inconsistent.

Similarly, the fabric of each story as related by our storytellers was woven with tales of clearly articulated parental expectations. Parents made it very clear what they expected of their children. The following was characteristic of the experience of most of the storytellers:

My parents were very concerned about who I ran with because I think in any neighborhood or community you're going to have some kids who are a bad influence on other kids and my parents didn't pick our friends for us but it was certain friends they didn't allow us to hang around and my parents didn't allow us to play with them or associate with them. I did have the close friends and the friends that I would frequently play with my parents had to know their parents and basically I couldn't go over nobody's house until I got permission from my parents and my parents would usually call their parents.

—Lanell

They (parents) would tell us this, "You know what's right and wrong. If you're with somebody and they start doing something wrong, you got to get away from them. If you go to jail, for anything, you are going to stay there. We're not going to come and get you out." And we knew they meant that so, we picked our friends. We wouldn't pick anybody that we knew would get in trouble.

—John

Our storytellers' parents also taught them the necessary skills needed to survive in a world where the likelihood of having one's self-esteem compromised was greater for the African-American. Some were taught not to venture into "white territory," say yes ma'am or no ma'am in addressing whites, not out of respect (as was the case in the African-American community and required in addressing your elders), but so as not to be considered insolent and bring trouble upon oneself. Others were taught to challenge the forces of racism, in whatever form it took, head on. The message was conveyed in a number of ways, but the bottom line was that race mattered.

Despite the extant reality, there was a persistent underlying theme of hope. Hope was the architect of dreams. Their parents possessed a sense that when hope dies one surrenders to the negative forces around you. When this happens progress is stifled and dreams dissipate into despair. A recurring theme among our storytellers was their recollection that their parents encouraged them to do better than they had. No matter how dire the circumstance, the message was clear. Here is one storytellers account:

See, my folks weren't educated. They didn't know too much about education because she (grandmother) couldn't read or write and whenever she had to sign documents, she took me along to read them and I signed her name to all the contracts. My grandmother wasn't educated but they always said back then that you're going to do better than I did. So I had that determination and I went and finished school. When school time came, you knew you were going. You knew it was school time and you knew you were going. There was no such thing that you were going to stay home. They made you go.

—Dave

This was a message of hope. It conveyed the subliminal message that such goals were possible to achieve, even in the world such as it is. It encouraged our storytellers to set goals and instilled in them the desire to want to be somebody. Parents, by their example, gave them the tools (the attitudes and values) to work with to accomplish these goals. Our storytellers painted a portrait of parents against a landscape of hardwork, persistence, consistency, self-discipline, and sacrifice. Their parents demanded no less of their children than they demanded of themselves. They practiced self-discipline and demanded it in kind. They lived by the values they taught.

While the level of formal education of many of the parents was limited, the extent to which education was stressed and valued was extensive. The refrain was always the same—with a good education, dreams need not be deferred. Education was perceived as the primary means of social mobility. Parents explicitly expressed the desire for their children to exceed their accomplishments. It was their charge that each generation should build upon the accomplishments of the previous generation until the pinnacle was reached. The value of education was communicated via the parents' support of the school, in general, and teachers in particular, who were perceived as respected professionals.

The role of parents extended beyond merely articulating expectations. Our storytellers gave detailed accounts of their perception of what their parents expected of them. Rules of conduct and expected behavior were clearly articulated by the parents. Failure to obey the rules or behave appropriately was frequently met with severe physical punishment. These were non-negotiable items and parental response was swift and consistent. Lorna tells a story that rings a familiar chord for many of our storytellers:

I was about fifteen years old. I received a very severe whipping from my mother. We had the National Association for the Advancement of Colored People and my father's best friend was the head of it, along with the minister from Halifax. They gave what you call a street dance where they close off so many streets and they have a band and the people dance. It was over at 12:00 o'clock, but my father gave me an order to be in the house at 12:00 o'clock. When I got ready to leave the dance, it started to rain. And my father's friend said, "You're not walking around the Commons this late at night. You wait for Rev. Oliver and me and we'll take you home." However, by the time they counted up all the money it was about a quarter to one when I got home. My mother saw me getting out of the car and saw a man. My mother started on me. I was angry because she did not give me a chance to tell her that I wasn't by myself. I was with Mr. Husbands, daddy's friend.

I think it was just instinct of my answering my mother back that when she slapped me in the mouth, I raised my hand. But I honestly to this day know I did not raise my hand to hit my mother. But as my father came in the door, he saw me with my hand up and he took off his belt and my father beat me until I was unconscious. It happened that my grandmother being older, took her a while to get down the steps. But then she whipped my father with the cane and took me upstairs. The next day, when my father told me to come downstairs (his friend had come in) and he saw me and he asked me what happened because my face was all swollen. There were welts all over me. He told my father he brought me home. And then my father felt so bad and so ashamed, he cried. And that's the day my father stopped whipping me. He never whipped me again.

But then, when you look back and you look at a man that had so many children and came from another country (West Indies) and was young. He did a wonderful job with us.

What is most striking about these accounts is that the storytellers did not interpret this type of discipline as abusive. They felt their parents were doing what parents were supposed to do. One can only leave to conjecture the reasons why. Perhaps it was their cognitive awareness of the association between family values and expected behavior. Or perhaps, the discipline was placed in the total scheme of things in which the storytellers felt they mattered and the many ways in which parents conveyed this message.

Discipline was clearly associated with specific acts. It was not a manifestation of a parent's displaced aggression. Therefore, the reader is cautioned against making moral judgments. While clearly the parents' actions may be offensive to the sensibilities of many, one must guard against that which distracts from hearing this subtle refrain. For it is not our purpose to judge the action, but rather to understand the action.

The value system was clear, for the die had been cast and discipline was a means of validating those values and encouraging compliance. The underlying philosophy of the parents tended to be that mistakes are the foundation upon which experience is built, and the role of corporal punishment was to ensure that a lesson learned was not soon forgotten. Every storyteller had vivid recollections of incidences that occurred during their childhood that resulted in the granddaddy of all whippings. They could recall with amazing clarity every detail. Most important, the lesson learned left an indelible mark on their psyche. Lorna's accounts was typical of the storytellers:

He wasn't a cruel father. He gave us everything. He wanted the best for us. He demanded certain things of us. As long as we did that, there was no problem. He demanded that we go to school. If we disobeyed the rules of the house, disrespected older people, disrespected our teachers, then we had to be chastised and his chastisement was whippings. Today, we call it child abuse. But in those days, it wasn't.

Joyce seemed to harbor tremendous respect for the values she was taught as a child, but the manner in which these values were taught and reinforced, with physical and verbal abuse at the hand of her mother, left her with a legacy of feeling inadequate and unworthy. Ironically, she harbored no resentment toward her mother. Here she offers an explanation:

She never uplifted me. She never encouraged me. I always walked with my head down. I loved my mother dearly. Even all of those whippings she gave me, like they call it child abuse today, I never hated her. I never thought of her as being an abusive parent. I knew she was doing what she thought was best for me. So, I always loved her.

Kangi viewed the severe punishment he and his siblings received from both parents from yet another perspective:

They were our parents, and we felt this was their responsibility. This was what they were supposed to do. So, we accepted it. Nobody was calling the police talking about brutality. Parents disciplined kids and that was just it. There was never any expression of animosity toward our parents, as far as discipline was concerned. My dad, we were frightened of him in that sense, but we weren't scared of him. If we did wrong, we knew what he was going to do.

Additionally, parents modeled the desired behaviors, values, and attitudes. This was particularly evident in the recurring theme of sacrifice. Many of the storytellers acknowledged a persistence and selflessness in the actions of their parents. It could be argued that it was this perceived quality that accounted for a lack of consciousness of life conditions that permeated many of the oral histories.

By their own account, our storytellers didn't feel poor, and despite lacking many of the amenities of life, they were happy. While we live in a society where many equate possession with happiness, where then lies the secret of their happiness? Perhaps the answer can be found in the quiet refrain of expressions of love, sacrifice, and caring. Our storytellers cast their parents in such a light. They knew that in the total scheme of things, they mattered. Here are typical accounts of such acts of selflessness:

You can be happy it doesn't always take clothes and food to be happy. If you never experienced all those other things. That's like a blind person. If you've never seen, you don't know what you're missing anyway.

—Dave

We didn't have steak everyday but the food we did have was the food that was necessary for us to have proper nutrition. My mother cut a lot of corners. She used to cut out coupons all the time. I feel that instead of my mother and father going out having a good time every once in a while, they sacrificed doing that to put money in the family budget so that we could make it. My father would go out and he had little skills to do craftsman work in terms of building little structures like doghouses or play houses or little birdhouses that people put in their trees to feed the birds. He used to do a little work like that. He would make very very little money. We certainly weren't living like kings and queens but we were living very comfortably.

—Lanell

The Depression had come on. My father had put a beautiful coat on layaway for her but things got so bad my mother let the coat go back. She took it off the layaway and took the part that he paid to buy clothes for us.

—Ernestine

Parental sacrifice was the personification of determination, hope (the belief that goals were attainable) and persistence in meeting challenges head on. It was as if they lived by the creed, Where there is a will, there is a way. They were possessed of a spirit untainted by the magnitude of the challenges that lie before them. These too were perceived as one more mountain to climb, rather than one more cross to bear. Mental attitude and physical fortitude would pave the road to success.

Another vehicle for the transmission of values, attitudes, and beliefs of parents and significant others was assigning the children certain household responsibilities, which provided them with opportunities to emulate and internalize these traits. It is interesting to note that the type of tasks assigned the children were essential to the running of the household and in many instances were not age-typical. For example, our storytellers recalled being assigned the task of cooking for the family, cleaning the house, doing repair work around the house, or working outside of the home, at a very young age.

While Juanita recalled painful memories of feeling as if her foster parents treated her and her brother as slave labor, as an adult she came to realize the benefits of that experience. Here is what she had to say:

My brother and I used to have a lot of talks together. We realized if we had been brought up by my mother, we probably would not have any of the tools our foster parents gave us. Even though they were abusive at times, they did give us tools to become independent people so we could take care of ourselves.

The significance of such responsibility should not be underestimated. One could argue that it established the importance of children in the household by assigning them meaningful tasks that contributed to the functioning of the household. Furthermore, such responsibility, it could be argued, is conducive to the conveyance of such values as self-discipline, dependability, accountability, and sharing.

The role of parents as sources of encouragement or role models weaved a common pattern in the fabric of the stories. Of particular interest was the role of the father. In most cases in which the household was intact (both parents living in the same household), the father was undeniably the acknowledged breadwinner. In these households, fathers were described as hardworking and perceived as caring by virtue of this trait. For the storytellers, love was not measured solely by physical expressions such as hugging or kissing.

The true measure of the man and his manhood was his dedication to his family. It was a dedication and caring that crept surreptiously into small innocuous moments or was reflected in actions so selfless as to go unnoticed by the casual observer. This was clearly evident in the words of George regarding his elderly father:

He doesn't say much but I know he feels something. He kept it within himself. He never said, this is my son (with pride) as far as I knew. But I had run in some race. It was really a hard race. I was so tired. I had really pushed and I was just exhausted and somebody was standing back down in all this crowd and I looked. "That's my father standing there." I don't know if mom knew he had left or not. He had come. He knew I was going to be in Chicago. He had come down to the Chicago Stadium. I don't know how he got down in the shower room and he said something like this, "You want to do this?" I don't know exactly but the point was, all the work I put on you, you never suffered like this [laugh].

Kangi would always remember his industrious and hardworking father, who lived for his family. It was from his strong work ethic and commitment to family that Kangi learned the true meaning of love and what it meant to be a man. He had this to say:

I liked the idea of him providing, because I understand he had been sick quite some time. But he didn't want to take days off because he knew he needed the money for us. He was a man who loved his family and I always felt that.

For the storytellers, love and caring found meaning in the actions of dedicated and committed fathers. Lorna's story strikes a familiar refrain:

My father didn't show love for his children like hugging us, kissing us, holding us. But there were so many things he did for us. I remember the baby sister that died. She had a tumor. If I remember her eye was removed when she was three years of age. And I remember my father used to come, get off the train (he was a conductor), get up in the morning and the clinic was a good hour walk from our house. It didn't bother my father. He would wrap the baby in blankets and say "Come along Lorna, we got to take your sister to the hospital." And my father is the one that would walk with me with the baby. And I remember while we were at the hospital, one of the worst storms in Canada had come up. Cars were coming, there wasn't any buses and my father was trying to walk through the storm to get us down the hill to the main street. A car stopped and the man and woman in the car said that they could take the two children and drop us at the bottom of the hill where we could go in to be warm. And dad said take them and he would walk.

He could sew and maybe some rich person would get rid of a coat or something to the Salvation Army. Daddy would take that coat and would make coats for all the children.

Other storytellers described fathers who were actively involved in parenting. Fathers were cast in the role of the disciplinarian and there were fond recollections of social activities with the father as the central figure. Not all of our storytellers, however, had such pristine tales to tell. All that glitters is not gold, for the mere presence of a father in the home did not ensure domestic tranquillity. None of the storytellers reared by a foster father or stepfather reported a loving relationship with the affinal relative.

The varied and complex relationships between our storytellers and their fathers suggest that such relationships viewed in isolation from other variables are not a reliable barometer for predicting the success of children. Additionally, not all of our storytellers were reared in two-parent households, either as a result of the death of the father or divorce. Consequently, some were reared in female-headed households.

An interesting variation on the theme of the role of the father in the family constellation came from the recollections of those storytellers whose fathers possessed an unusually strong work ethic or whose fathers worked at occupations that kept them away from home frequently or for extended periods of time. This, too, impacted the storytellers in different ways. For some, there was a sense of fatherlessness, while for others the intermittent or extended absence of the father was overshadowed by the quality of the relationship when the father was present and the nature of the bond between father and child that been previously forged and developed over time. In both instances, however, the father's presence in the household was consistent. In the final analysis, neither the composition of the family constellation nor the pattern of father absence had a negative impact on the ultimate success of our storytellers.

This is an interesting observation given that much of the social pathology that envelops inner-city African-American communities has been attributed to the disproportionately high incidence of father-absent households. Juvenile delinquency, mental illness, poor academic performance, and an assortment of other social ills have been attributed, in large measure, to this phenomenon.

However, other authors provide a counter-argument to this position. Austin (1989) examined four theoretical concepts that in his opinion render fallacious assumptions regarding the negative impact of father-absence. They are as follows:

1. The absence of the father puts the family in dire financial straits requiring the mother to seek employment outside of the home, leaving the children without proper adult supervision and resulting in behavior problems.
2. The absence of the father creates economic hardship on the family that may force older siblings to leave school to seek employment to help support the family.
3. The absence of the father results in low income and low educational attainment.
4. The absence of the father deprives children of a male role model necessary for proper psychological development.

The stigma of illegitimacy, divorce and abandonment have an adverse effect on children. It is on this point that he challenges the negative impact of father-absence on aspiration and achievement. He holds that father-absence does not have a negative impact on groups for whom this phenomenon is not statistically deviant. In other words, among groups where the rate of father-absence is high, such as among blacks in the United States, the Caribbean, Brazil, and the Caribbean coast of Central America, there is no stigma attached to father-absence. Therefore, the negative impact is nil. Among groups or in communities where father-absence households are the norm, the negative consequences are attenuated.

Other American studies have yielded similar results. Herzog and Sudia (1973) looked at the relationship between father-absence and school achievement and found no deleterious effects on lower-class black children. Wasserman (1972) studied the relationship between father-absence and school achievement and attitude among low income black boys from a housing project and similarly failed to find a negative impact of father-absence.

Heatherington (1983) and her colleagues also failed to find a negative impact of father-absence on the achievement of black children. Father-presence was salient as it related to sex role development. However, they went a step further, noting that the deleterious impact of father-absence was abated by the presence of surrogate parents or other relatives in the household. They concluded that father-absence has a negative impact on achievement only among groups where middle-class values are the accepted norm. Greenberg and Davidson (1972), in their study of low income African-American students, similarly failed to substantiate a deleterious effect of father-absence on achievement. In a comparison of high and low achievers, they found father-absence did not differentiate between the two groups.

For the storytellers who were reared in or were themselves the female head of a household, the absence of the father was attenuated by strong family networks, friendship groups, or community support. Even in intact households, there was frequent mention of the strong role of the grandmother. Others spoke of the support provided by neighbors or friends. Additionally, those who lived in extended family settings benefited from financial assistance and emotional support. Lorna held particularly strong views on the subject:

I can't go along with that a family has to have a man in it or that a child has to have a father in it for that child to grow up into being a useful citizen. That's not true. I believe in the extended family. All of these children have grandparents. They have uncles. They have their male teachers in the school. I've seen children in my hometown (in Halifax) come out to be doctors and their parents couldn't read and write.

For the male storytellers, the significant impact of sports on their lives cannot be overstated. Sports brought them into contact with coaches who served as positive male role models. For others, teachers or community leaders served as significant others filling a void in their lives. The role of these individuals in the lives of the storytellers attest to the power of one. One person can make a difference. Most important, the difference can be embodied in something as innocuous or ephemeral as a word of encouragement, an act of faith in the ability of another, or a show of concern. Perfectly timed, meticulously executed, generosity of the spirit can save lives. The potency of the power of one suggests that the presence of a father is not as important as the presence of an individual who fulfills this role and all that it engenders.

In conclusion, the family unequivocally stands as the primary purveyor of values, attitudes, and beliefs that shape our destiny. It is the root of our being. It is within the family that we come to be who we are. The deeper the root, the stronger the tree. Our storytellers affirm this truth. The more firmly grounded in their families and the values it embraced, the greater their resiliency in combating adversity.

10

It Takes a Village to Raise a Child: Support System

As we traveled through the pages of the lives of our storytellers, we encountered in each chapter central figures that left an indelible mark on their lives. Like the pieces of a mosaic, each possessed a unique character and impacted the life of the storyteller in an equally unique way. When the pieces are assembled, a portrait of our storytellers emerges—the magnificent creation of the influences of the many who made a difference in their lives. The portrait is cast against a landscape that traverse time and place. These significant others were encountered at various stages of the life cycle and in different settings. Home, school, church, community, and the workplace was where relationships blossomed and were nurtured.

These significant others were the role models. It was in their shadow that our storytellers basked. It was these individuals they aspired to please and emulate. They inspired hope and helped them envision possibilities beyond the horizon. They were living proof that it could be done. By their words, deeds, and actions, they confirmed the belief that despite one's circumstance, one's hopes and aspirations need not be mere pipedreams. The importance of the presence of role models is indisputable. Some are by nature skeptics of this concept and for youths, in particular, showing them the possibilities is a much more convincing and potent reality than merely telling them of the possibilities.

Andrea is a social worker with a master's degree from the University of Chicago. She attributes her success in meeting the challenges of teenage pregnancy, a failed marriage, and of being a single parent in large measure to her mother, who she witnessed fight many battles of her own. The role Andrea's mother played in her life as a significant other and role model is typical of many of the storytellers who shared their life histories:

I don't think that if my mom had of done what she did, I'm not convinced that I would've finished school. She was kind of the role model and she did it. Even if she had of just encouraged me, I don't know if that would have been enough. I mean they (family) were encouraging us all the time, but I actually saw her do it. It's pretty hard to live kind of like in the ghetto and realize that there is another world outside of your little world and think that you can be successful. You know it's like people can tell you and you see people but in my mind it was like I could never do that. But I see that you can. You can be anything you want to be.

They are trying to survive in whatever way they can and that's a problem. So I think one of the basic things is, they've got to have more role models that can be with them quite often. I mean seeing somebody on TV or reading about somebody in the papers, that's not going to do it. We've got to be with these people. We've got to share with them in situations and help to guide them.

—James

The importance of role models and significant others is a chorus that has been taken up by many. Barbara Shade (1983) studied the social success of black youths, focusing on the impact of significant others in their lives and concluded that the issue is not who socializes the child as to the accepted norms, values, and customs of society but rather that someone who holds emotional significance for the child assumes this responsibility. Consequently, the presence of traditional socializers and role models (mother, father) is not the sole requisite for social success.

Similarly, M. S. Maehr (1974) joins the chorus in his book, *Sociocultural Origins of Achievement,* with a focus on affiliative response. That is, the child consciously strives to behave in such a way as is pleasing to the referent person. It is this desire to please the significant other that motivates the child to conform to standards of expected behavior.

Clearly, this was a familiar refrain in many of the stories. However, the stories further suggest that conformity to expected behavior was also derived from a clearly articulated familial value system. Value clarification was enforced via strict discipline and internalized.

While the significant other was a recurring theme in the oral histories, not all of the significant others were parents. As each story unfolded, the significant other was cast in many roles. Many of the male storytellers, in particular, were positively impacted by participation in various organizations, such as clubs, sports teams, or fraternities. Other storytellers were strongly influenced by members of their extended family or individuals in the community.

Numerous other authors have compiled quite an extensive list of significant others that extend beyond the immediate family.

Individuals, groups, or agencies that serve as significant others include, cousins, aunts, uncles, peers, adult friends, white society, and even the media.

Edward's involvement in the Edgewater Boys Club attests to the powerful influence of club membership on self-esteem and one's sense of belonging:

There was a club in Edgewater called the Edgewater Boys Achievement Club. This was like a boys club and Rev. Johnson was the founder of this organization along with Mrs. Hopson and a number of other people who I can't remember now. Mr. Chappel and some others that lived in Edgewater started this organization just to keep boys off the street and doing things constructive to keep them out of trouble. There were crafts which they would make wallets, belts and play games and go on trips. So I got excited and I wanted to join but I was too young. But they saw how enthusiastic I was about it and allowed me to come in at nine. We participated in all the parades and we wore military uniforms.

For our male storytellers, membership in fraternities had an empowering effect and it heightened their sense of racial identification and pride. Languishing just below the surface was a subtheme that affirmed that if you allow people a sense of pride and dignity, you give them a reason to fight adversity. Teach them who they are and they will struggle to remain true to themselves. The message is not new. It was the battle cry of the sixties and echoed through the halls of time in such slogans as "Black is beautiful" and the Rev. Jesse Jackson's "I am somebody" and "If you can conceive it and believe it, you can achieve it."

Affiliation with various other social service–oriented organizations tended to have a similar effect. Here is James's perception of the impact of an organization of which he is a member:

I was introduced to a national organization called the National Conference of African-American Males. Its headquarters is located at the University of Kansas and I became a member. This organization advocates the need for role models for African-American males. It advocates trying to save the African-American male.

Steve found membership in his college fraternity heightened his sense of racial identity and pride and broke down the social barriers that divided African-American male students on the basis of geographical location, socioeconomic status, or past group affiliations. It was an empowering experience.

For our female storytellers, group membership had a similar effect. It was in the group, communing with other females, that they encountered positive role models, those of a kindred spirit who knew, personally, their pain and their struggle to free themselves from the shackles of racism and sexism. The submissive posture of their gender would be abandoned and replaced with a quiet, yet determined reserve, to define one's own destiny. They relied on each other, collectively or individually, for the emotional support needed to make their dreams a reality.

The African-American family has been the topic of considerable discussion and debate from the antebellum period to the present. Unfortunately, much of the discussion and debate has centered around its disintegration and associated social pathology. In focusing on the negatives, the positive dynamics that take place in many African-American families have gone unnoticed. It is as if the dominant culture views the African-American family with tunnel vision. Because the family structure does not always mirror that of the dominant culture, it has come to be viewed as somehow defective.

Our storytellers illuminate the very positive dynamics of the African-American family. Therefore, the potential and importance of the African-American kinship network warrants further discussion. The extensive kinship network of black families, in the form of extended families or relatives who do not live in the household but provide a consistent and reliable support system, ameliorated family crises such as financial or emotional problems and provided child care (McAdoo, 1977). Additionally, this network has the potential to perform other functions, such as socializing the young as to the norms, values, and expectations of society, setting standards for acceptable behavior, and providing an environment in which children could develop positive self-concepts.

Nancy Schlossberg (1984) takes a more global perspective emphasizing the multiplicity of factors that impact an individual's ability to confront challenging life situations. She concludes that each life stage brings with it challenging situations and identifies four primary sources of support in assisting individuals to meet these challenges head on. They were: (1) their intimate relationships, (2) their family units, (3) their network of friends, and (4) the institutions or communities of which they are a part. These sources of support figured significantly in an individual's ability to confront challenging life situations and was a source of motivation. Numerous other studies offer support to the significance of support systems in ameliorating stressful situations.

Clearly, in each of the oral histories, the success of the storyteller's triumph over adversity could not be attributed to any one factor. In each case, there were numerous variables working in tandem. Others have found greater family cohesiveness among individuals who more effectively dealt with stressful situations than those with lesser family cohesiveness (Lowenthal and Chiriboga, 1975). Similarly, the survival of people in Nazi concentration camps was related to the degree to which they were able to become a part of the group during the first few days of their arrival.   Once a part of the group, the social dynamics of the group functioned to provide the individual with the necessary information for survival, such as protection, advice, and information.   Significantly, the group assisted the inmate in maintaining the foundation of perseverance—self-worth (Dimsdale, 1976).

This finding raises interesting speculation regarding the degree to which this same principle may apply to African-Americans trapped in the ghettos of major cities around the country.   Could the key to surviving social oppression be the degree of social integration into a group and the group's role in teaching the individual survival skills and reinforcing their sense of self-worth?   Clearly, the refrain that maintains the cadence of the life experiences of our storytellers would support such a conclusion.   No matter how bad the times, one could always count on the family or the larger community to weather the storm.   There was strength in unity.   The pain of the one was felt by the many.   Consequently, sharing meager resources was done with a willing spirit.   There was always room at the table for one more.   Our storytellers paused and stared nostalgically at the past to caress moments of caring when people lived by the creed, I am my brothers keeper.   A time when "we care" was more important than "welfare."

The uniqueness of the African-American mother has been captured in many studies.   She has been credited with, among other things, influencing school performance (Gurin and Epps, 1966).   Others who have sought to identify the factors that enabled lower-class minority males to achieve social mobility and escape the ghetto, despite their socioeconomic status and neighborhood environment, found that the common thread that bound these individuals together and insulated them from the deleterious effects of ghetto life was the presence of a significant other, in the person of their mothers (Ross and Glaser, 1973).

The role of the mother as a significant other in influencing the behavior of our storytellers cannot be overlooked or underestimated. The pivotal role of the African-American mother in family dynamics is deeply rooted in the past.   She has withstood the test of time and remains the bulwark against environmental conditions that threaten her brood.   When the family constellation is altered by death, divorce, or abandonment and hard times lurk in the shadows, she rises like a phoenix from the ashes and reclaims that which is hers.   Our storytellers' accounts abound with tales of her strength and courage and her "take no prisoners" attitude in rearing her children.   When the world seemed foreboding, she stilled the waters.   She was the steady flame that burned, refusing to relinquish her glow to the ill winds that blow.   Irrepressible in their mission to mold and protect, such were the mothers and grandmothers of our storytellers.

James, a retired high school principal, recollected of the role his mother played in his life and it is typical of many of the storytellers:

My mom was always available. So she became somewhat my role model to a degree because she was always there for me and she did everything she could to bridge any gaps that might have been created as a result of the lack of my stepdad being around. We had a void there my mother tried to fill with my father (stepdad) being missing because of work. She encouraged me to be involved with all school activities. She encouraged that and then she would come to see me perform. She encouraged us to be involved in church. She was always encouraging us to do those positive things. She was the one that encouraged us and that gave us the initiative to go on and get involved in a lot of things.

She was always talking to us about getting an education so that we could get on with our lives. She was a big help. She was very instrumental in my really being able to get through high school because the area where we lived there were a lot of gangs and those kinds of things and I did at one time belong to one of those gangs which was involved in a lot of fighting with other gangs. But through my mother's conversations with me, the talking and what have you, I was able to not go to the extent of getting myself involved with any illegal situations that would have caused me to be incarcerated. And then when I got to junior high school and high school, sports was the other thing that really changed my whole attention about life and things.

The significant impact of the black mother on her children has long been historically documented and most scholars would contend that this holds true today. From the antebellum South to the present, the strong attachment and protective bond between the black mother and her children has been unbroken by time and circumstance. Consequently, black mothers exert commendable influence on their children (Nobles, 1974). This refrain is taken up by Stinnett and Wallers (1973), who concluded that the bond between black mothers and their siblings was stronger than between European-American parents and their children, and that the primary source of affection for black children was their mothers. The black mother has also been credited with influencing the aspirations of their children (Kandel, 1974).

Clearly, mothers and grandmothers played a significant role in the success of our storytellers. They were generally described as hardworking, selfless, encouraging, caring, always being there, and in many cases the disciplinarian. They were the purveyors of values. Even the severe physical punishment administered by their hand was interpreted by many of the storytellers as deserved because the punishment seemed to fit the crime. The crime was usually a violation of the values that would produced good character and contribute to becoming successful, morally upright children. Discipline was interpreted as caring. Mothers were respected, and their mere presence seemed to provide a sense of security. By their example or explicit guidance, mothers motivated their children to meet the expectations they set for them.

Significant others also have been shown to impact occupational aspirations. One study showed that for black females, their mother, followed by the person in the occupational role they aspired to achieve someday, close friend, siblings, relatives, teachers, father, school counselor and family friends, exerted the greatest influence on occupational aspiration. For black males, the order of influence was the person holding the job, followed by parents, teachers, siblings, friends, other relatives, school counselor, and family friends (Pallone et al., 1973).

Shade (1978) noted a clear pattern of relationship between shifts in who the significant other is and the age of the individual. Upon entering college, freshmen were asked who in their environment most influenced their educational and occupational aspirations. Peers, teachers, counselors, friends, and siblings were at the top of the list and parents were last. This suggests that as children's social experiences expand beyond the home, the more parent-independent they become, the more other nonfamily members acquire significance in their lives and influence their behavior and aspirations. An interesting twist to the preceding conclusions came in a study of a sample of eighteen- to thirty-five-year-olds who had already experienced educational and occupational mobility. When asked who exerted the greatest influence on their aspirations, mother and father were at the top of the list.

In retrospect, adults who are established or are experiencing positive returns educationally or occupationally, take a panoramic view of their lives and with renewed vision, reassess the role of their parents in their lives (Scanzoni, 1971). In general, this held true for our storytellers. They reassessed many of their parents' actions. They understood even more clearly than before their parents' underlying motivations. There was a common refrain of a desire to please parents and of a sense of gratitude for the many sacrifices their parents made on their behalves.

All of the storytellers succeeded in fulfilling their parents' expectation that they exceed their ambitions and accomplishments in life. Their stories suggest that a major influence in their desire to achieve was derived from values taught in the home and was reinforced by exposure to positive role models and successful peers. Also, families tended to live in close-knit communities where neighbors shared similar values. This is clearly indicated in the following oral history:

Around 37th Street where we [lived], all those families, the parents, we weren't unique, our parents. Well, some of them would drink and some of them would do this but by and large all those youngsters went to college. All of them went, most of them went to Wendell Phillips High School. There's the Smiths and there's Mosley Braun, her parents lived right next door to us.

—George W. Jr.

For many of our storytellers, not just one individual in the family constellation served as a significant other. There was clearly a sense of the collective impact of the family in assisting children in developing survival skills and the mental attitude for academic success. Nobles (1974) makes a similar case when he argues that the historically close-knit and supportive black family is the source of survival skills and achievement motivation.

Many of our storytellers were part of an extended family setting or lived in close proximity to other relatives who impacted their lives. The role of the grandmother in the extended family household was particularly relevant, for it was she who served as the primary caretaker of the children while the parent(s) worked. Oftentimes the grandmother was the central figure in the household, providing support for family members within and outside the immediate household. It was not uncommon for single parents to live with their parent(s) or for adult children to assist their younger siblings to achieve certain goals. This was clearly evident in the following oral history from James: "And I talked to my two sisters and mentioned to them that you all go on and get yourselves together and when I get out of school, I'll help you get through."

Of particular interest is the role phenomena, other than persons, that act as significant others such as white society and the media. The media have a powerful impact on the formation of social attitudes among African-American youth (Leifer et al., 1974). Keller (1963) provides some clues as to the process whereby the media has impacted the lives of lower-class youth. He found that lower-class youth watched more television than other groups; consequently, he concluded that television became an influential force in their lives. Not only is there a higher incidence of television viewing among African-American youth, on the average, they engage in more radio listening than other Americans (Greenberg, 1972).

The reach of these seemingly innocuous phenomena cannot be underestimated. Given the right environment, they insidiously interject self-doubt and the acceptance of stereotypical images of one's group. The media, particularly television, are masterful purveyors of cultural norms, values, and social attitudes. To the extent that the media portray certain groups in a less than desirable light, media's influence can have a debilitating impact on the perception these groups have of themselves. Numerous other studies have come to similar conclusions. The media's negative and stereotypical portrayal of blacks influences their perception of self and their position in the social order (Surlin and Dominick, 1971). The way in which blacks are portrayed in the media sends a subliminal message to black children that they are not capable of achieving educationally or economically. Furthermore, blacks are depicted as docile, nonassertive, intellectually inferior, incompetent, and inherently different from whites. Black youths internalize these stereotypical images of self, thereby short-circuiting the conventional value system and adapting a value system consistent with their extant reality (Cartwright, 1975). In this regard, the role of peer group acquires special significance.

The experiences of the storytellers confirmed the impact of the media on self-perception. They were generally cognizant of the portrayal of their race in the media, as well as the role of the media as a purveyor of cultural values.

Steve was most cognizant of the power of the media to shape race perception. This is what he had to say:

Then there is the electronic media. I go outside my door, I see drug dealers and gangbangers. I don't know why they are there. I can only repeat what I hear white people say on TV. They're black inner-city youth. I go back and watch my TV and all I see on TV when it comes to a crime is, this black man committed this crime or this black this or this black that. Then, I turn on National Geographic. All I see are Africans jumping around in grass skirts. Not being taught anything about my culture, not seeing it as beautiful, you see this as primitive.

Two fifteen-year-olds that immediately went into drug dealing and came up with the exact car that the Mack had in the movie. The point that I'm getting at is, the media and society paint a picture of where you should be to be accepted but they never show people positive ways of getting there. The only means they show of getting there is negative.

—Gregory

However, the impact of the media did not yield the same deleterious effects on our storytellers. Clearly, they were not negatively impacted. Their stories revealed a number of variables that may have been efficacious in attenuating the negative impact of the media on self-perception. Plausible explanations are high self-esteem nurtured in family settings where they felt valued, preparedness (being socialized by their parents as to the realities of being African-American in a white world), exposure to positive role models, the belief that goals were attainable, buoyed by parental encouragement and support and accountability. Here is what two storytellers had to say:

As my parents told me, "Don't worry about what somebody else says. You know who you are. You have your own set of aspirations and go forth, the sky is the limit."

—John

[My mother] said we should always be fair. We should always be honest but stand up for your rights and don't run from situations.

—James

Peer groups validate perceptions and reinforce the behaviors that evolve from these perceptions (Perkins, 1975). Through peer group affiliation, lower-class black males learn the vernacular, mannerisms, and behaviors of their subculture. Most important, peer group affiliation results in estrangement from parental and community locus of control and influence (Clark, 1969). Others have focused on the more practical functional role of the peer group. While conceding the formidable power of the medium of television as a purveyor of the views and perceptions of the larger society, they also acknowledged the role and influence of peer group street subcultures in providing instruction in surviving life in the ghetto (Leifer et al., 1974).

However, because black males may seek success through nonconventional means does not mean they are not achievement oriented. What it does mean is that they reject the institutionalized means of achieving cultural goals (i.e., those things which society says we should all strive to achieve or have deemed important). They did not reject the cultural goals and differed from others only in the preferred method of achieving their goals (Merchant, 1976).

For our storytellers, peer group affiliation and the family value system were conjoined. Their stories confirm the strong relationship between the two. There was an emphasis on selecting peer groups that mirrored their family's values. In fact, many explicitly stated that their parents insisted on their socializing with those of similar values. Additionally, the impact of deviant peer groups was attenuated by parental control, exposure to positive models, the desire to reach a long-term goal and the availability of socially acceptable outlets for adolescents, such as organized sports or other community programs. The following from Ernestine was typical of the recollections of most of the storytellers: "I knew better than to take up with people who weren't [like us]."

SCHOOL AND COMMUNITY

Much of the discourse on achievement and aspirations has centered around familial processes and dynamics. Few have examined the interaction between such extraneous variables as school and community. One notable exception was the work of Slaughter and Epps (1987) who focused on home environment and achievement of black children. They placed the issue within an historical context to clearly articulate the process whereby schools replaced the family and assumed the function of formal education.

They argued that "as the economy became increasingly industrial, the family had less of the collective wisdom needed by each new generation to participate competently in society. Schools gradually replaced families as the primary source of this wisdom. Black Americans' early and determined struggle for formal education, including the perception that this was a key, if not the key, to attaining full citizenship in America, has been well documented" (p. 4). Additionally, increased immigration and migration after the Civil War contributed to shifting the responsibility of education of children from the family to the school. This shift was a politically motivated response to the need for a literate citizenry. The continued rapid rate of social change created conditions that have required educational institutions to assume functions that were once clearly the responsibility of families.

This blurring, overlapping, and redefining of functions has created a schism between parents and the school. Their relationship is far too often adversarial rather than cooperative. Clearly, more work is needed in the area of ameliorating the relationship between parents and the school. There is a deficit of knowledge of how family environment interacts with schooling for different ages and subgroups within society. Indubitably, both are significant factors in academic achievement.

Conversely, our storytellers relate a different reality. The threads of their stories weave a pattern of strong parental support of the school and of adult authority in general. Education was valued and associated with the parents' desire that their offspring should attain a higher status in life. This was clearly evident in many of their stories:

I was in third grade. I had a friend that was sitting next to me and I took a tack and sat the tack in his seat so that me and my friends could laugh when he sat down. It was out of fun, not to hurt anybody. After the teacher was notified that I did it, of course the teacher called my mother and she came up there immediately. When I got a note that my mother was there, my mother requested that I come to the office and when I came to the office I didn't get any reprimand from the school but my mother asked the principal would it be alright if she could whip me before the class. It wasn't a brutal whipping but she did hit me a couple of times with a small paddle. I think the reason I cried was not because of the pain but the embarrassment that I put on myself. And to this day, I'm glad that mama did that because I never had any problems with acting up anymore in my classroom because I didn't want to be embarrassed again. And I think the main reason that mama did it, not to embarrass me but was to let me know that it's not right to do things like that and of course if you do not comply with rules and regulations not only in school but also out in the world you will get punished.

—Lanell

Parents were always involved with the school. They stayed involved with the school. They made sure that everything that was supposed to be going on in the school went on. The schools were good too. They were concerned about educating kids.

—James

[My parents'] whole idea was you had one job and your job was to go to school and get good grades. That was our job and if you didn't do it then you were in trouble. So, if they got any report from school that you didn't do your homework or you were late or you were talking in class or talking back to the teacher, we were in trouble.

—John

Families do not exist in a vacuum. They exist within the social context of the community and the community within society. Therefore, the role of the community and larger society as they impact the family cannot be overstated. At another level, Slaughter and Epps (1987) considered the role of the community and larger society as it impacts the family. In their study on reading readiness they argued that "the home environment's role as educator to the child is interdependent with many other, continuing, changing, and frequently competing roles that it fulfills. While we have some idea of what would be beneficial to children's early reading, we have little idea of how these processes manifest themselves in the roles enacted by culturally and socially different families in their natural settings" (p. 7). This suggests the need for an in-depth look at these environments to develop strategies to assist parents and educators in working together to develop and implement reading intervention programs.

The role of the community in the lives of our storytellers was significant. Most were from close-knit communities. The values of the families were reflected in the community. There was pride in the family name. Children were cautious not to behave in a manner that would bring disgrace to the family. It was also in these close-knit communities that children were perceived as everyone's concern. Their stories echoed a common refrain in which neighbors reprimanded each other's children for wrongdoing and informed their parents who responded in kind. So effortlessly was this theme played out that the casual observer may have assumed a consanguine relationship between child and adult. Such behavior on the part of neighbors was part of the natural order of things. Generally speaking, it was not perceived as overstepping one's boundary and consequently was not met with resistance. There was a sense of community, trust, and shared responsibility that bound neighbors together. Children were valued and deemed everyone's responsibility. There was pride in the family name and children were cautious to behave in a manner which reflected family values. The following recollections were typical of the storytellers:

It was like a block party and there was a lot of communication going on. The thing is that other people would watch out for you. If you did something wrong, they would know about it, your parents would know about it. When another adult saw you doing something wrong, they could tell you to stop. It wasn't that people would get mad or anything. It was a lot of good networking going on.

—Andrea

The neighbors there were like family. Everybody knew everyone on the block. The kids knew one another and we were just like sisters and brothers basically. The people on the block were so close. The neighbors were so close that if one of us got out of hand, then that particular parent, if they saw us getting out of hand would give us a spanking. And after they would spank us, they would notify our parents and when we got home, we got another spanking. Everybody helped raise everybody's children.

—Lanell

We were brought up to respect our neighbors. The way we were brought up was, we were never allowed to answer any other adult. And even though my father was away, we knew he knew what we were doing while he was gone because when he got off the train, which was like downtown Chicago to come here to Country Club Hills, by the time dad got home, if I'd did anything wrong and the neighbors seen it, dad knew it. If we skipped school, mom may not have known it but somebody would see us on a day that they knew we should have been in school. And they called my father Patty, "Patty, Wednesday, I saw Lorna at about 10 o'clock. She wasn't in school. Was she going somewhere for your wife?" And so, we had to put up with neighbors telling on us. And there was no such thing as, answering back a neighbor or saying a neighbor was lying on you. There was respect for your elders.

—Lorna

Strong support of the schools and education in general were grounded in this sense of community and shared values. The following recollection was typical of the experiences of many of the storytellers:

We had a lot of proud people in the community. They were very proud and those people were doing everything they could to make sure that their kids got a good education.

—James

So strong was the sense of commitment to the youths in the community that some of the storytellers recalled community members providing scholarships for college or assisting students in other ways. This was clearly evident in the life histories of Edward and Kangi.

The potential for the community to positively influence student achievement has been confirmed by others. Ward (1971) studied the home language environment of low-income black children and found that the underlying philosophy that governed the adult community's interaction with children was that children should be seen and not heard. Children were not encouraged to join in adult conversation, and adults, generally, did not engage children in conversation. The study found few child quality-enhancing products, such as educational toys, in these environments, and the children received minimal guided language instruction. It concluded that as human language development takes place within the confines of the extended family, community, peers, siblings, and other relatives, there is a need for intensive study of these groups to ascertain precisely how they influence early language development.

The life experiences of our storytellers, however, warranted a different interpretation. While many of the storytellers spoke of children being forbidden to participate in adult conversations, in the African-American community this was part of a value system that emphasized respect for adult authority. Similarly, while many of them may have lacked store-bought–educationally enhancing toys, it could be argued that the absence of such toys tended to enhance their creativity and communication skills. They frequently alluded to the joy and pleasure of childhood games, sports, and making things. Indubitably, the computer has taken center stage as a conveyor of knowledge and instruction in the home as well as the classroom. However, this new technology by its very nature limits the need for interaction between people in a learning situation.

This recollection of one storyteller is indicative of the types of activities that were, in the absence of educationally enhancing toys, conducive to the development of cognitive as well as social skills:

We had lots of books because I loved to read and still do and we always had lots of books. We played hopscotch, jumping rope and things like that.

—Ernestine

Similarly, the strong religious orientation of many of the families of the storytellers drew them together for Bible study or regular church attendance. Consequently, while they may not have been engaged in adult conversations, they were clearly a part of the social settings. Within these settings values were transmitted, rules of decorum established and lessons taught. One could even argue that there was considerable communication between adults and children. This was clearly illustrated in Gregory's accounts:

My grandmother was a minister and she was deeply involved in the church and Jesus Christ. One of the pastimes I spent with my grandmother was, she would read me biblical stories.

When we were little and able to read, my father would make us come in the room with him. He would get the Bible and sit down. He would make us read scriptures from the Bible. Then he would always tell us what the parable meant. He could always explain the parables in the Bible.

—Joyce

Language development acquires added significance as children become indoctrinated into the formal educational setting with its white middle-class orientation. Under these circumstances, the success or failure of black children is, to a degree, dependent upon their ability to understand and emulate the language patterns of the dominant culture.

Brice-Heath (1982) conducted an ethnographic study of language development in a lower-income African-American community in a southeastern city. The school system had been recently desegregated and teachers and students were experiencing difficulties communicating with each other. A study of the problem revealed differences in how questions and interrogatives were used in the children's community and how they were used by the teachers. She concluded that within the children's community, questions served a different purpose. In school questions were used by adults to create understanding by analogy.

Consequently, contrary to the rules of language for the dominant culture represented by the teachers, amorphous, unexplained comparisons were perceived by the children as legitimate responses. Teachers, on the other hand, used questions as a stimulus for interaction with their students about some specific phenomenon. Brice-Heath also observed that in the community, adults did not direct questions or comments about the child to the child but rather to a third person. Teachers, conversely, would address questions or comments about the child directly to the child. Other significant differences in the manner in which adults in the community communicated with children that were diametrically opposed to the way in which teachers interacted with the children were also noted.

This implies that while lower-income black children possess verbal skills, the norms governing when and the acceptable manner in which they may verbalize their thoughts differ from middle-class norms. Consequently, for teachers to effectively meet the needs of these black children, they must understand the norms governing language socialization in the black community and incorporate this knowledge into their teaching methodology.

The accounts of our storytellers provide support for this position. The family value system of many of the storytellers required that as a sign of respect, children not participate in adult conversation. Also, children were admonished not to talk back, as this was viewed as a challenge to adult authority. The recollection of this storyteller was typical of the experiences of most of the storytellers:

We were brought up to respect our neighbors. The way we were brought up was, we were never allowed to answer any other adult. If we skipped school, mom may not have known it but somebody would see us on a day that they knew we should have been in school. And they called my father Patty, "Patty, Wednesday, I saw Lorna at about 10 o'clock. She wasn't in school. Was she going somewhere for your wife?" So, we had to put up with neighbors telling on us. And there was no such thing as answering back a neighbor or saying a neighbor was lying on you. There was respect for your elders.

—Lorna

Our storytellers shed new light on the dynamics of student-teacher interaction and interpersonal relationships. Clearly there was an undercurrent of feelings and emotions that transcended, which typically accompany these roles. The ability of teachers to reach students was grounded, to a large degree, in their affective responses to students. This theme emerged from the shadows when our storytellers were asked to recall teachers that influenced them the most. The clarity with which they recalled events and circumstances attests to the impact of the relationship between teacher and student on self-esteem and the long-term effect these teachers had on our storytellers.

The following account is representative of the perception of the vast majority of the storytellers:

One of my teachers that had the most impact on me was really in elementary school and she was a white music teacher. Mrs. Glass developed what she called a boy's chorus. We traveled everywhere. We were singing the classic songs. She was very sincere. She was very patient and she was the one that got us exposed by having us perform all those concerts in different parts of the state. She was a music teacher and she wasn't required to do anything but teach us music but she went further.

—James

The impact of teachers on our storytellers was not limited to early educational experiences. The potential for teachers to impact, either positively or negatively, the self-esteem, level of achievement, and aspirations of students spans the life cycle and educational settings. From preschool to the adult education classroom, the power of teachers to build or destroy confidence, encourage or discourage hopes and dreams is undeniable. In this sense, teachers really do touch the future.

The affective responses of teachers are clearly noted in the following accounts:

They [college instructors] were black for the most part. It was like a family. They were totally committed to our total development. They would be at all of the activities, take you to their house for dinner. They were always around with us. I mean after work hours you would see them on campus because Kentucky State is such a beautiful place.

—James

Miss Deloach basically took me under her wing, took me by the hand, just showing me everything that I needed to do. She was just a real caring person and I honestly believe that she would have been in that library trying to help us if they would have cut her salary. She was just that type of woman. Seemed like she was sincere in her job and she just wasn't going through any motions. She tried to do what she could to help us to be effective.

—Lanell

The teachers our storytellers identified as having the greatest influence on them were characteristically caring, patient, going beyond the call of duty, and perceived as taking a personal interest in them. They attended to the affective as well as cognitive needs of their students.

Not all of our storytellers, however, harbored such fond memories. For many, the waters were turbulent, flooding their senses with painful memories. Some recalled negative experiences with teachers that were grounded in racial/cultural issues. A grating issue was the storytellers' perception that white teachers and counselors tended not to encourage them and interacted with them based on stereotypical images of African-Americans. Additionally, white teachers, in general, were not perceived to take an affective interest in them. Some of the storytellers perceived approval by white teachers as dependent upon the degree to which the children approximated white standards of behavior and appearance. Consider Lorna's interpretation of her school experience:

When I got to grade seven, I had a teacher, Mr. Parson. He was white. We had no black teachers and the majority of our teachers were from England. I think it goes back to the same thing in the United States. He was partial to the whiter-skinned children. If you were black and you were yellow-skinned and you had good hair, he would push you. He was mean to me. He used to embarrass me. I think he learned real quick that our father didn't play with us and he seemed to enjoy getting me in trouble with my father.

Though the fairest girls in the group were my best friends, he treated me different than the way he treated them. I definitely got a dislike against him. I think that may be what stopped me from wanting to go on to the high school.

Our stories are woven together yielding a vibrantly colored pattern of cooperation between home, school, and community. Education was highly prized and teachers respected. Kangi best describes how teachers were perceived:

You have to understand during the time I came up to be a teacher, particularly a black teacher, was an honored profession. Teachers are not honored today like they were then. We just respected a person that was teaching us and the kids responded. If somebody responds to you, you're going to give your best.

I saw teachers as having power. They were pretty much their own bosses, which I felt I wanted when I grew up.

They had an effect on society, and I wanted to be able to contribute to that. That's how I perceived my teachers.

—Juanita

Home, school, and community were of one accord, tuned to the same frequency, thus creating an environment for children in which the same message was being conveyed. Reality dissonance was not as problematic. What was true in one world, the home, was also true in the others, school and community. The experience of this storyteller was typical:

While you were in school, the teachers were your parents, you might say. Whatever they said or wrote notes home, the parents sanctioned what they did. There was none of this business, "I'm going to come up here and let you have it." You probably heard of that old rule back then, if the teacher said you did it and somebody else said you did it, the teacher gave you a whipping and when you went home, you got another one. See, we lived during that kind of discipline back then. You didn't sass them. You didn't disrespect no one. You always gave everybody respect.

—Dave

MENTORING

Within these worlds—home, school, and community—the importance of mentoring relationships was clearly illustrated in many of the stories. Many of the storytellers either acknowledged the significance of the role of a caring other in their lives or perceived the need for such an individual. The role of the mentor, however, extended beyond mere caring and encouragement and being someone to emulate to including purposeful guidance to mold the individual to achieve certain goals.

The social context in which the mentoring experience occurred included home, school, and community. Additionally, the mentoring experience was perceived to be beneficial at various points in one's life stage development. The mentoring process was set in motion by the mentor precipitated by an interest in the storyteller based on personal qualities, life situations, or a natural outcome of the social environment.

There was the case of Ernestine, now in her late seventies, who recalled being a young married mother, whose own mother died when she was barely in her teens, who was counseled by the older women in the community:

Because I didn't have a mother, there were two ladies, Lucille Wright's mother and Mrs. Tyrese would always come and see about me. They would come and see about me and help me with the kids and see that everything went OK with the kids. [When someone got sick], they knew what to do with their old remedies. They helped me down through the years with the kids. We got along quite well and the kids were happy.

—Ernestine

For other storytellers, mentoring relationships evolved from the adult education experience, as illustrated here in Lorna's story:

[I had] just separated from my husband. Didn't know where he was because he had left and didn't support the children. I didn't know how I was going to look after the children. Through an instructor from South Suburban College, she encouraged me to take the Constitution. That was the way she got me into the school. Then she encouraged me to get my GED. Well, after I got to the GED school, Theta Hambright, who was the Dean of Community Education, became my mentor. She started pushing me to finish and get the GED. Then she started pushing me to go ahead and get my A.A. All the time, I kept saying, well, I'm not college material. And I couldn't picture a junior college. I knew nothing about junior colleges. I only knew about university. So then once I started going to school and I transferred and went on to Roosevelt [University], I guess I became a professional student.

Well, after I started going downtown to Roosevelt [University], many, many people helped me. I didn't have the money for car fare. One of the teachers, Mr. Presley, he also had a second job at the University of Illinois. He went out of his way every time I got off of work, I was a teacher's aide then. So, the Dean helped me. She got me a little job that would give a little money then to give me my car fare. And he would drive me directly from my job to the doors of Roosevelt University and drop me there. So, that meant I only had to have my car fare to get home.

Encouragement and the mentoring experience was particularly significant for one physically challenged wheelchair-bound storyteller:

As far as me being in school, my friend, I call her my mother because she's my mother away from home, Debbie Moller. She's the secretary of Student Support Services. She has really been a mother to me. Like when I'm really down and there's no one for me to talk about it to. Sometimes, in order for me to release my feelings or the fact that I'm hurt, she'll hug me and encourage me to go on. Because she's working on her bachelor's degree. She says if I don't give up, if I'm not going to give up, don't you give up. And she knows what it's like to be disabled because she was in an accident herself. And she says, "You let me hear somebody putting somebody else down with a disability. I'll come running after them with my cane." And when I talk to her about giving up, she's like, "I'm going to come after you with my cane and I'm going to beat you. You'd better not give up. Do you realize how far you came." I mean when I went to South Suburban, I was there since 1987 because when I was at Purdue-Calumet it was like, I was just a number. I wasn't treated like a person. I was just a number and whatever I told my student support service counselor over there, she told everybody in that office. It's like I had no confidence or whatever to trust her or anything. That's what makes it so hard for me to trust people.

—Yolanda

The life-changing potential of mentoring relationships struck a resonant chord in the stories of Edward and Gregory. Mentors were hearld as shepherds in the night, assuredly watchful, providing a cloak of emotional and sometimes physical safety. They were the personification of hopes and dreams. It was through them that our storytellers could catch fleeting glimpses of the future.

The significance of the mentoring experience has been documented in a number of studies. Labov and Robbins (1969) confirmed the positive influence of mentors on males between the ages of sixteen and twenty-five. Bridgeman and Burbach (1976) noted that the influence of a significant other had a greater bearing on achievement expectation than prior success. These findings give rise to some interesting speculations. One could conclude that it is very possible for individuals to turn their lives around at any point during the life cycle. The point at which these special individuals entered the lives of our storytellers and the impact they had on them was not constrained by time.   The significant variable therefore becomes who or what serves as the stimulus for change and not as previously thought, the point in the life cycle that the stimulus is introduced (i.e., early childhood).

For other storytellers, however, the bend in the road to success was not as easily identifiable. Having come to a fork in the road, the chosen path was often dictated by forced circumstances or a product of the dynamics that accompany each stage of the life cycle. Neugarten (1976) makes a case for the latter in identifying three shifts characteristic of the middle years— *increasing interiority,* which is characterized by introspection. The individual is more concerned with the inner self than the outside world; *reversal in directionality,* in which individuals conceive of time in terms of that which is remaining as opposed to time since birth, they realize that life is finite; and lastly, *personalization of death.* Here there is a realization that death is an inevitable conclusion of life (p. 17).

Schlossberg (1984) concluded that " whether the reassessment of the self and the world that usually accompanies a major transition (at whatever age it occurs) leads to greater self-confidence or diminished assurance, the result is a renewed assertion of identity" (p. 22). Clearly, then, during the middle years whether an individual, through reassessing his or her life, decides to take stock and make changes for the better or sinks deeper into an abyss of despair is an issue.

Ironically, negative life events may have positive consequences. The term "transition state" refers to periods in our lives in which we must address such issues as tension, fatigue, emotional trauma, or seek out new support systems (Weiss, 1976). Dealing with such issues creates personal as well as relational changes. A case in point may be the loss of a job. Most individuals would consider this a maximum stress-producing phenomenon accompanied by depression and anxiety. However, this situation may be the stimulus needed to push an individual to explore new and better career opportunities, a step that in all probability would not have been taken had the loss of the job not occurred.

Moos and Tsu (1976) found that individuals vary in their responses to life transitions. For some individuals a transition may be processed as an opportunity for psychological growth, while for others it may be the catalyst for psychological deterioration.   The problem then becomes one of identifying the variable(s) that account for why individuals who experience the same life transition react to it differently.   Within the framework of this inquiry the question becomes why is it that for some individuals a traumatic experience or a life transition may be the impetus for positive change and for others a source of further deterioration? Why is it that for some individuals these variables (i.e., life transition or traumatic experience), result in surmounting barriers and for others they create additional barriers?

The answers to these questions rise to the surface when we break down the barriers that separate our world from that of the other and permit ourselves to see with renewed vision the world as they experience it. As their stories unfold, our storytellers offer numerous examples of triumph over adversity. However, these experiences derive meaning from the social context in which they occur. Hearing their stories, one could conclude that diametrically opposed responses to similar trauma could be attributed to any one or a combination of the following:

1. How the individual interprets the situation. You might call it the "I'll show you" or the "When life hands you lemons, make lemonade" mentality.
2. The internalization of fortifying values and attitudes acquired during the formative years and parental child-rearing practices. Our storytellers shared stories of hope, persistence, commitment, and sacrifice as exemplified in the lives of their parents.
3. The support of significant others and visible role models.
4. Goal fixation (having a goal, a point of focus into which physical and emotional energy is directed).
5. Preparation (knowing what to expect).

Our storytellers' life experiences lend indisputable support to the significance of mentoring in goal attainment and the sometimes positive consequences of negative experiences. Each story was driven by a pulsating beat breathing life into the adage, "when life hands you lemons, make lemonade."

Yolanda, a wheelchair-bound college student, had this to say:

What people find so amazing about me is when there is something negative going on in my life, I turn around and I try to make it positive. I don't care what anybody says to me. I'll tell anybody that has a disability, you have something special. Don't let anybody tell you what you can and cannot do. You can either use it to help you overcome the obstacle or use it to hinder you. There were times when no one was around to bring me to school and I would take a cab. One day I was unfortunate to get a cabdriver who just didn't care, who had no concept of people with disabilities. I noticed that when I was getting out of the cab and he was setting my chair up for me he didn't actually set it up for me. He threw it on the ground. He threw my tray on the ground. He threw everything that was associated with my chair on the ground. That's why I'm so focused on learning how to drive and get my own car.

Thus far we have addressed issues as they pertain to the individual as a separate entity. A shift in perspective suggests yet another dimension of the phenomenon of triumph over adversity from the perspective of collectives.

Using this frame of reference, the critical pedagogy paradigm and work of Paulo Freire (1970) on "conscientization" and Jack Mezirow (1981) on perspective transformation acquires relevancy. Freire's concept of conscientization evolved from his experiences working with socially and politically oppressed groups in Latin America. He concluded that the persistent oppressive conditions under which these people lived were perpetuated by their lack of critical consciousness of the underlying motives that guide the dominant hegemony who controlled their lives. Without having reached the level of critical consciousness, the oppressed are ill-equipped to confront the issue or take definitive action. According to Freire, critical consciousness (i.e., an awareness of the forces that control one's life), results in empowerment. When individuals feel empowered, they are then primed for action.

Reality is socially constructed. Consequently, our beliefs and values reflect those of the dominant culture and as such serve to advance the agenda of the dominant culture. Political and social policy, therefore, do not always serve the best interests of minority groups in the population. The interests of those that are not members of the dominant culture would be better served if they were to critically examine the underlying assumptions of the values, beliefs, and social and political policies that they have come to accept as true and factual. Only when this is done can these individuals be empowered to effect social change (Freire, 1970).

Given the historical castelike status of African-Americans in society, the critical pedagogy paradigm provides another piece to the puzzle of triumph over adversity. One key to closing the doors of social oppression is for groups to ultimately question the status quo and band together to effect social change. The Civil Rights Movement of the late 1950s and the 1960s and, most recently, the Chicago School Reform Movement, which gives parents a more active role in the education of their children through the establishment of local school councils, and the tenant management concept of some of the Chicago Housing Authority facilities are examples of people questioning the extant reality and effecting social change.

In conclusion, our storytellers stand as living testimonials to the adage that few people achieve success without the help of another. Each had the good fortune to stand in the presence of a caring human being who acknowledged their self-worth and potential and assisted them in molding their future.

11

Light a Candle and Curse the Darkness: Resistance

RACE PERCEPTION

The issue of race, in varying degrees, impacted the lives of our storytellers. Clearly, each acknowledged a sense of being set apart by virtue of their racial heritage. The realization of racial inequality tended to intensify with increased contact with others outside their immediate environment. Racial inequality was sensed superficially during childhood. Many of the storytellers acknowledged knowing that blacks and whites lived separate lives based on segregated housing patterns and school attendance. However, at this stage in their development, they interpreted this fact as the norm. No one in their immediate environment challenged de facto segregation. Consequently, the worlds were quite separate and as such there was no standard against which to measure or discern disparities in lifestyle and life chances. Kangi made this observation:

But you accept it as normal really. You got used to it, so you didn't complain. My dealings with white people only when I went downtown. In the neighborhood, you never saw them, except maybe an insurance man, or they would make deliveries police.

However, as Kangi's world expanded beyond his immediate environment, it would be his strong self-image that could be credited with his courage to challenge the forces of racism as he encountered them. He affirmed, "I never thought white people were better than me, for one thing."

Adolescence was, characteristically, the time period in which most of the storytellers first began to consciously discern disparities in treatment and how they were perceived by members of the dominant culture. It would be in the world of work that this awareness and incumbent repercussions would reach a peak. It is interesting that the initial heightened awareness should occur at a time during human development when the search for identity is a major issue. It is also a time when social interaction and the need to belong acquires greater significance for the adolescent. The repercussions in regards to an assessment of personal worth is clear.

Many of the older storytellers, in particular, were cognizant of the socially construed perception of self-worth based on race at a very early age. Here is a clear illustration:

I thought race relations was terrible. In the South where I came from, it was really, really bad because there you had the KKK factions. They'd burn crosses in the neighborhood and the black folks would shake in their boots. You had separate but equal schooling and you had lunch counters you couldn't go to. You were on the back of the bus. You name it. They'd come in your neighborhood, do whatever they want to. Molest your ladies and kill your young men and throw them in the rivers and you never found them. And they had the slogan, "Stay in your place."

I'll never forget. The police one day on the street corner struck my grandmother, without a cause, on her arm and there again a lot of times they'd get out of order and you'd have to take it or they'd just haul you off to jail and do you any kind of way. They did what they wanted to. If you went to court, the court was so rigged against black folks, you would lose the case anyway.

—Dave

For the most part, it was in the classroom that our storytellers were first confronted with the issue of race perception and personal worth. Many recalled incidents that left an indelible mark on them. For most, their response was a strengthened resolve to disprove the stereotypes. The following was typical of their experiences:

For the most part, most of the administrators and most of the counselors were all white. I was real motivated; so even though my scores said I was an average student, my grades were A's and B's and probably a few C's. One of the things I can remember that was real significant for me was that the counselor, I guess I took the ACT test and the counselor said that my scores were mediocre but that I should go ahead and be a secretary. He saw my grades were real good in that area and that's all I should do. So I went home and I was crying to my mother because I was upset at what he said. So when he told me that, that made me feel real bad. My mom came up to the school and told him that "You'd better not ever tell my daughter what she cannot be. If she wants to be a doctor, you better encourage her to be a doctor. I don't care about these test scores and what they're saying." That really made me feel good.

—Andrea

Edward gives this account of his reaction to a high school counselor who discouraged him from pursuing a college education: "The fact that they told me I shouldn't go to college and this and that, I decided that it would be my challenge to go to college." The deleterious impact of race on the lifestyle and life chances of black Americans has been documented by many.   Social, political, and economic conditions have estranged many black males from traditional values and propelled them into an abyss of despair as manifested in the disproportionately high rates of drug and alcohol abuse and criminal behavior.   The most devastating consequence has been that many respond in ways that suggest they have not only accepted but internalized society's negative images of them (Strickland, 1989).

Similarly, others argue that many African-American children reject the traditional value of education as a vehicle for social mobility due to the historical castelike status and incumbent restrictions on their minority group (Ogbu, 1981). In other words, they do not perceive education as being efficacious in achieving the American Dream or gaining entrance into the mainstream of society.

Hare and Castenell (1987) join the chorus noting the role of structural inequality as a significant variable in the evolution and perpetuation of underachievement of black youth. They contend that "while acknowledging the relative underattainment of black Americans the relative academic and economic failure of black Americans in the American social order is functional, if not intended, given racism and the differential distribution of wealth, power, and privilege in the social structure" (p. 101).

While some of our storytellers wrestled with the issue of racial identity due to differential treatment, only one clearly attributed his induction into a deviant subculture as a direct consequence of such treatment. The characteristic response, however, was to defy the stereotype.

Race still matters. Its roots are buried deep in the past, refusing to yield to the winds of time. The tenacity with which it grips the past and darkens the future is a theme eloquently played out in Derrick Bell's *Faces at the Bottom of the Well* and Ellis Cose's, *The Rage of a Privileged Class*. We are unable to escape its shadow. Even when we walk facing the sun, its shadow follows us. Given this reality, and as in Andrea's case, many of the storytellers were successful in their attempt to repel the deleterious effect of racial stereotyping. They were bolstered by encouragement from significant others, had the desire to please a significant other, the sheer will and determination to accomplish a goal, and the exposure to positive role models, and in general a positive nurturing environment in which they developed good self-esteem. This was their shield against despair.

SELF-ESTEEM

The significance of the role of positive self-esteem in the lives of our storytellers cannot be overstated. It enabled them to resist allowing adverse social conditions or circumstances to define or limit their aspirations or challenge their perception of self.

Lorna expressed pride in the fact that her father instilled in her and her siblings a sense of racial pride at an early age:

I knew black history. I knew about blacks having black kings, black queens. My father had a very large picture of Emperor Haile Selassie on one side of the fireplace and on the other side was a big picture of the Queen of Judea. So we knew as we were growing up that we came from a background of kings and queens. We were taught that by my father. So we've always had pride in our blackness.

For the male storytellers, in particular, sports played a very significant role in directing their energy into socially acceptable activities with very positive ancillary consequences. Diminished self-esteem and participation in deviant subcultures that may evolve from racial stereotyping was abated by participation in sports. For the vast majority, sports provided them with coaches that served as positive male role models, as well as the opportunity to be acknowledged for their skill on the court or playing field.

Participation in sports had a transforming effect. It was a means of channeling energy and releasing frustrations that could have short-circuited into an inner-directed destructive force (frustration implosion). The vestiges of this energy gone awry is visible in swagger of the gangbanger who dominants the street corners of inner-city ghettos, the stupor of the addict as he slips into a contradictory world of painless agony, and the broken spirit of children of neglect, futures lost, stolen, and strayed. There was also the potential for this destructive force to be directed outward toward others (frustration explosion), leaving in its wake soaring crime rates. Sports was empowering, giving our storytellers a sense of control, as well as the opportunity to interact with other males in an organized activity governed by rules of participation.

The almost mystical effect of sports in the lives of young African-American males is evident in the success and increasing popularity of midnight basketball leagues. These leagues are the latest addition to the arsenal of anticrime programs. What they provide for the participant is a sense of belonging, a goal, structure, and discipline.

Our male storytellers spoke with pride of their athletic accomplishments. Kangi and Gregory recalled the very strong impact of sports on their lives, as it bolstered their self-esteem, served as a deterrant to involvement in gang activity, and was a buffer against being victimized by active gang members:

I never belonged to a gang. I was an athlete. I was a good ballplayer and they knew me by that, Pee Wee Joe Louis. So when you're an athlete they call you by that and they don't mess with you gangwise.

—Kangi

Sports kept me out of trouble. It really did. Sports kept me in school. When I got angry or had a problem, even a math problem, I would go out and play basketball or something like that by myself and then I would come back and look at the problem and it was easier to deal with.

—Gregory

For the female storytellers, education was frequently the seed from which self-esteem blossomed. Carole notes the role of education in bolstering her self-esteem and extending her vision of the future. This was a common scenario for the female storytellers:

When I got divorced, I went back and got my high school diploma, went to college and then got a trade. I began to be somebody having some sort of status.

The ancillary socializing role of sports participation has been well documented Participation in sports provides a forum in which boys learn culturally prescribed sex role behaviors, such as toughness and competition. The role of sports in the lives of impoverished young African-American males is even more far-reaching (Lever, 1976).

Clearly, for our storytellers, positive self-esteem proved to be a valuable weapon in their arsenal against adversity. It enabled them to face the challenges before them and set increasingly ambitious goals.

THE VALUE OF NEGATIVE EXPERIENCES

Without exception, each storyteller could recall some incident in his or her life that held the potential to seriously compromise personal self-esteem and aspirations. What seemed to shield them from falling prey was their interpretation of the incident. Their response was grounded in their perspective of the incident in relation to their perception of self.

Joyce credits something as innocuous as her excellent penmanship to an emotionally piercing incident while in grade school. She similarly credits other accomplishments in her life to the emotional hardships evolving from her learning disability.

Carole shared an incident, as a young girl, that was instrumental in motivating her to set long-term goals and expand her aspirations. Carole's mother and grandmother both worked as domestics in the homes of whites. During special holidays, as a child of twelve, Carole accompanied her grandmother to work to assist with the cleaning, cooking, and serving. It was the humiliation of this experience that strengthened her resolve to be the master of her own fate.

The response of Carole and Joyce to such incidents was typical of the storytellers. Clearly, there was the tendency to view potential obstacles in life as stepping-stones rather than stumbling blocks.

As their stories unfold, they offer other important clues to identifying the factors in the adult years that may precipitate overcoming the odds. Their stories resonate with strong elements of persistence, hope, having a dream or goal, a significant other, and encouragement by someone who believes in your potential. Most important, it addresses the most problematic issue of identifying the specific incident that prompts individuals to say "I have had enough" and to begin their quest to turn their lives around.

Clearly, for many of the women a change in life circumstances precipitated by divorce was the motivating force to explore options not previously considered. Lorna found herself a single parent, as a result of divorce, struggling to raise two children. Things took a turn for the worse when she suffered a heart attack that prevented her from working to support her family. She was forced to join the welfare rolls. Finding the experience an affront to her sense of dignity and self-esteem, she struggled to regain her independence:

One of the biggest reasons I wanted to get my bachelor's degree is, I have to be honest about it, is I took a dislike against my caseworker. She belittled me. I had to go for the first time in my life over to the welfare office. At that time it was in Harvey and I sat in a room with maybe two hundred people waiting to be served. To me, they were treated like they were dirt. They weren't even being respected as being a human being that was just down on their luck at the time. She didn't care whether I was sick or not. I'll never forget the time I had an appointment with her and I wasn't able to make the appointment. I was in the hospital in intensive care and she stopped my check. When I got on my feet, I told her I wasn't going to tolerate this. There was no way I was going to go through the rest of my life having to hold my head down with the pride that I had in myself. I was going to become somebody. I felt I was somebody. I was determined that I was going to use that welfare check for two years. Every time I got a report card or my grades mailed to me, I'd look at them and I'd start checking off, I'm getting closer to those sixty [semester hours].

For one storyteller, the underlying motivation for change was the desire to please a terminally ill parent via a reconciliation of the values taught him as a child. For another, the crisis point was an emotional bottoming out and the realization that his options were limited (i.e., change or die).

The common thread in each story wove a pattern that clearly articulated the significant role of the family in the socialization process and specific child-rearing practices as conducive to the development of coping mechanisms and how one defines a situation or circumstance.

Much of the literature on the phenomena of triumph over adversity has failed to focus on the interaction of variables that impact the phenomena. What was lacking was an ecological perspective. *The American Heritage Dictionary of the English Language* defines ecology as the science of the relationships between organisms and their environments. Human behavior is defined within a social/environmental setting. Research has shown a relationship between changes in environment and behavior and performance. The ecological perspective suggests the importance of studying the interaction between the individual and the environment, in the inquiry into triumph over adversity. Clearly, as the two are *interactive*, changes in one will result in change in the other. Consequently the ecological perspective suggests that the individual and his or her environment should not be studied as separate entities.

As we travel through the pages of the lives of our storytellers, we are offered a clear illustration of the complexity of the issue. Their stories paint a vivid picture of the multitude of variables that act in concert to impact their lives.

GOAL FIXATION

The tenacity with which the storytellers confronted situations that conflicted with their perception of self had the ancillary effect of assisting them in defining and clarifying their goals. Resistance formed the foundation upon which goals were formulated or pursued with resolve and determination. This theme flowed melodiously from many of the oral histories and was clearly illustrated in Steve's story.

As gangs began to form and his longtime friends began to succumb to the pressure and join opposing gang factions, Steve found himself walking a very precarious line, that which required him to maintain friendships on both sides while not becoming intricately involved in the activities of either group. The choices were limited. You either joined a gang, which provided you with protection, or you had to isolate yourself from the gang as a means of protection.

The consequences of either action are disturbing. To join a gang puts one at risk of physical harm, via confrontations with rival gangs or involvement in criminal activities that frequently led to incarceration. The choice not to join creates an imposed social, psychological, and emotional isolation. You either preyed on others, or you were preyed upon. However, the focal point for Steve that enabled him to maintain this balance was his desire for an education.

In effect, he had a goal which gave direction to his life, and most important, one that he believed he could achieve. Steve said: "I was actually ready to join that gang, but I thought about it and I knew I wanted my education beyond any of it."

Juanita came to the realization that no matter what your past history, success is always on the horizon. However, one must change their perspective to see it. With these words, she clearly makes her point:

I just had to come to the conclusion that no matter where you start from, you can always make it better if you want. You can sit there and cry the blues, and you can blame things on other people. You can realize a dream. If you set a course, if you set a goal that you can be somebody and you can accomplish it, if you continue to work hard and believe and just keep doing it step by step.

The relationship between a positive self-concept and goal setting was clearly illustrated in the oral histories. Our storytellers had either acquired positive self-concepts during the process of socialization in their formative years or learned to feel good about themselves as a result of encouragement from significant others, role models, or past success in achieving an important goal.

In conclusion, resistance was a significant factor in the storytellers' success in conquering adversity. Resistance was buoyed by their perception of self, desire to accomplish goals, and their interpretation of social reality. Particularly in regards to the latter, they were not disarmed by negative situations. On the contrary, such situations served to strengthen their resolve and determination.

They refused to allow themselves to be swallowed in an abyss of self-pity, recognized it served no useful purpose, and transcended it. Gregory summarized this sentiment best with these words: "If a person can actually take the worst thing that could happen to them and see that as an event, but not their life, I think everything else comes with that."

12

Faith Can Move Mountains: Spirituality

Indubitably, religious conviction was a formidable force in the lives of the storytellers, the source of which could be traced back to the early socialization process. In many of their homes, religious instruction was deliberate and purposeful. It physically brought family members together, calling time out from the daily routines of life, and in so doing validated its significance and importance. The following are some accounts of how religious beliefs and instruction were transmitted:

We could never go to the show or anyplace until we had been to church on Sunday. My father was an usher at Progressive Baptist Church. We were very religious oriented. I remember, on Sunday morning, listening to Wings Over Jordan, a gospel group. As we listened, Mama would comb our hair and what-have-you. We all went to church together.

—Kangi

When we were little and able to read, my father would make us come in the room with him. He would get the Bible and sit down. He would make us read scriptures from the Bible. Then, he would always tell us what the parable meant. He could always explain the parables in the Bible.

—Joyce

My grandmother was a minister, and she was deeply involved in the church and Jesus Christ. One of the pastimes I spent with my grandmother was she would read me biblical stories.

—Gregory

Religious practices took a fundamentalist bent. It was expected that religious teachings would be manifest in the way one lives life. Church attendance was often mandatory and not viewed ritualistically. Church was where values were consistently validated and reaffirmed.

In many instances, the church was part of an important social support network. It came to the aid of those in need; it was the arena in which leadership skills could be developed; it offered comfort and sustained hope and faith. Religious instruction, reinforced by the home and church, provided the blueprint for life. It was the embodiment of hope, faith, and charity.

Edward gives this account of the role of the church in his life:

Rev. Johnson was a minister. He added a very strong religious connotation to the club, and we would sing gospel songs and visit churches, hospitals and other organizations and sing gospel. Then, Rev. Johnson formed his own church outside of the Edgewater Boys Achievement Club and I became a strong member in the church. All of these activities were leading me toward greater involvement in the church. I became a Sunday school teacher, later a Sunday school superintendent, and the next thing I knew I was a church musician. I remember one day, I had to play the piano, had to teach Sunday school and then had to preach; all that happened one Sunday. The pastor didn't show up and the word was sent to me to preach and there I was.

Such a strong and consistent force was religion and the church in the families of many of the storytellers that their teachings seemed to be effortlessly internalized. It was simply a way of life. This was clearly evident in responses of Kangi:

I did drugs and taught Sunday school. I always went to church, I didn't care what I did. I'd go to church high but I went to church. I've always been a Christian. In spite of the fact, I wasn't what you'd call a good Christian because I did a lot of things contrary to what I know God would want me to do, but my Christian upbringing was just in me. I don't believe I've ever hated anybody.

This chapter in the lives of our storytellers suggests that their own cognizance of the impact of religion in their lives was not fully realized until they reached adulthood or began to face many of life's challenges. Their stories give substance to the meaning of strong religious conviction and abiding faith. For many, it was their religious faith that calmed the raging storms of adversity. It was this faith that was the source of their strength to persevere, to be optimistic under the most trying of circumstances, and to deal with fears of the unknown. Like a seed that lies dormant and takes root and blossoms only when its season has come, strong religious conviction and faith journeyed from the depths of their inner selves to shield, protect and insulate.

It was Joyce's strong religious conviction that sustained her through the traumatic loss of her job. Here is how she assessed the situation:

I think God knew. I think God had a hand in this, because he knew I was getting very tired of that job. I was getting weary because I just didn't want to work there anymore. God sometimes takes something away from you, but he also replaces it with something else.

It would be Carole's strong religious faith that motivated her to take a risk and start her own business and deal with her son's homosexuality:

I still didn't like working, punching a clock for somebody else. I wanted something of my own. It wasn't until this situation with my son, and God spoke to me and said, "If you abide in me, I will abide in you and all things will be given unto you. But, you've got to obey me and do my will." When I went out and attempted to do what I'm doing now, I had no idea how I was going to do it, where the money was going to come from. There were weeks when I didn't make any money, but my bills got paid every week. Every month, my bills got paid and it was just on the faith.

Some of the male storytellers credited a solid religious foundation and Christian upbringing with having saved them from themselves. Clearly, for these individuals the rediscovery of their religious roots was the road map back to normalcy, creating a peace within themselves and life in general. While incarcerated, Gregory had this religious relevation:

I was just about on my sixth month and for some reason or another, I had the feeling that I was going to get out. I prayed to God in my own little way and I did acknowledge what I should be about, and a dream came to me. It told me that I was going home on September something, go back to school.

In surveying his past, Kangi acknowledges the power of God to change people:

I've often felt that I should have not ever been named a minister, but I know what God does with people. He changes them. He takes people from the guttermost and makes them what he wants to make out of them. I've looked in the Bible and read about many people with lives similar to mine. Sometimes, I wonder how in the world God could forgive me for all this stuff and use me in the way he has.

Among the storytellers, there was a prevailing sense of God as Protector; that no matter what the situation, by the grace of God they would emerge victorious. Gregory found this to be the case as he attempted to skirt the impending dangers lurking in the shadows of prison life. Here is how he accounts for the protection he received from other prisoners: "But because of the love and respect for the type of person they knew I was, they buffered me from possible danger. Later, I realized that was God protecting me."

Joyce's sense of Divine protection and intercession sustained her through a long period of unemployment, as illustrated here:

Ever since I lost that job, I have not struggled one day. I have met all my bills. In fact, I paid them on time, when I couldn't pay them on time when I was working. I paid them on time and always had food. I never had one day's struggle, and I know God is looking down upon me. I know he sees my struggle, and I know he understands. I know I'm going to work. So, I still have that feeling nothing is going to bring me down.

Juanita acknowledges the role of religion in filling the voids in her life and enhancing the total quality of her life. She had this to say:

I became a Christian, and I feel that has helped to fill a lot of the other voids that were in my life. It's helped me build self-esteem. The spiritual side of my life has enhanced my whole life. When you're feeling down and depressed, pray, God lifts you up. I feel he has answered a lot of my prayers. I couldn't have made a lot of decisions or accomplishments in my life without the help of God.

Religious conviction was empowering. From this belief sprang forth the tenacity to weather the storms of life and keep the doors of hope open. Their religious conviction was also their blueprint for living life. The significance of the role of religion is clearly illustrated in the accounts of these storytellers:

[God] is the center of my life and without him I couldn't do anything. I have learned you cannot control people, places or things but what you can control is yourself. There are days when life can't always be sunshine. There has to be some rain but whatever you do, God is still with you.

—Yolanda

I was just determined that I wasn't going to live like that. But [I] was powerless to do anything about it. See, you're powerless to do anything about it until the Lord comes in. He empowers you to live right. God himself empowers you to live right. Those kind of desires I don't have now. After coming to know the Lord, there's room for forgiveness and there's not room to hold grudges or hate or anything on that order. There was quite a change there.

—Dave

Clearly, religion figured prominently in the lives of the storytellers. In large measure, one could argue that the strength of their religious conviction could be attributed to early childhood experiences where religious values were taught and practiced in the home. Their lives attest to the power of religion and a belief in a higher Being to pull one from the depths of despair and provide a bridge over turbulent waters. It served as an anchor, repelling the force of the storm and a beacon in the night, guiding to safe harbor those who strayed.

Variously, their belief in God was attributed to enhancing the total quality of life, protection and intercession, perseverance, change in behavior, forgiveness, and courage to explore uncharted paths in life. They tended to live by the creed, faith can move mountains.

13

Summary, Conclusions and Implications

While each storyteller's life experiences were unique, their stories revealed many common threads that were woven into the fabric of their lives. Their stories provide strong support to the argument that these commonalties played a significant role in their success in overcoming adversity. They were family roots, support systems, resistance, and spirituality.

FAMILY ROOTS

Strong family values. Of all of the common threads inherent in their stories, it was strong family values that formed the primary source from which the others sprang. It was the foundation upon which hopes and dreams were built. In retrospect, all of the storytellers could clearly associate the values taught them by their parents, during the socialization process, with their attitudes, beliefs, and aspirations. Clearly, respect for adult authority, responsibility, accountability, and a strong work ethic were paramount among the values taught.

Strict discipline. Almost without exception, strict discipline was an integral part of the socialization process. It appeared to be a means of clarifying values. By today's standards the very physical nature of the discipline the storytellers experienced at the hands of their parents would be considered abusive. However, our storytellers did not interpret it as such. They clearly saw the connection between the discipline and its purpose. Consequently, they interpreted discipline as caring. They perceived discipline as part of their parents' responsibility to ensure that they grew up to be the kind of person their parents wanted them to be. This is not to say they welcomed this type of punishment, but they clearly understood the underlying motivation. Most important, parents modeled the behavior they expected of their children. Also, discipline was consistent. It was not sporadic or intermittent. Violation of rules of conduct or other prescribed behaviors or expectations were responded to in a consistent manner.

Parental sacrifice. Though lacking many of the amenities of life, our storytellers acknowledged being happy and not feeling poor. While there were stories of second-hand clothing and meals consisting of bread, butter, and sugar, they contended that they were very happy during these lean years. As their stories unfolded, clues surfaced that could possibly explain this perception. Among them was the fact that they indicated they felt loved and valued. They perceived their parents making sacrifices on their behalves. Their parents never afforded themselves luxuries at the expense of the children. They were cognizant of the fact that their parents were doing their best. Parents were perceived as hardworking and industrious.

SUPPORT SYSTEMS

Cohesive communities. For the most part, our storytellers acknowledged growing up in communities where children were valued and considered everyone's responsibility. Their communities exemplified the African adage that "it takes a village to raise a child." Neighbors could discipline each other's children without fear of negative repercussions. Family values and community values were of one accord and both supported the school. There was a sense of stability, self-respect, and pride.

School. Virtually all of the storytellers could recall an African-American teacher that left a lasting, positive impression on them. These teachers held certain traits in common. They were perceived as going beyond the call of duty, taking extra time with students or exposing them to things outside the curriculum. They were very affective, caring about the child as a person and not merely someone to be taught.

They were master craftsmen. They were the potters that molded the clay. Rather than leave the vessel in its simple utilitarian state, they chose to embellish it, give it the kind of aesthetic appeal that would cause others to reflect upon its beauty. So it was with their charges. They helped them to see the spring-well of creativity and potential that lie within them.

Sports. For the male storytellers, sports played a significant role in directing their energy into socially acceptable activities. In this arena, they could be somebody. Many explicitly credited their participation in sports to repelling the lure of gangs. Sports also brought them into contact with positive male role models and provided a forum to display their athletic prowess and gain recognition among their peers.

Organized activities and membership in formal or informal groups, in general, were vital in creating a sense of belonging, cooperating with others to accomplish a goal, and relying on others in the group for support and encouragement. There were rules of conduct and discipline and membership enhanced one's sense of pride.

Role Models. Our storytellers' parents were their most important role models. They recalled with astounding clarity how their parents influenced their behavior. In general, parents were perceived as hardworking, industrious, caring, and making sacrifices on behalf of the children. In addition to parents, they found role models among their teachers, coaches, or other adults in the community. Role models were essential in projecting a sense of hope. They were the mirror into the future. They were living proof that goals were attainable and more important they defined the possibilities and stretched the imagination. The subliminal message was that no matter the extant reality, one could beat the odds. It was their contention that in order for those who are struggling against the odds to succeed, they must have examples before them. It is important that they see for themselves that it can be done.

Significant other. Our storytellers' lives were enriched by the presence of someone in their lives to whom they felt particularly close. Someone they could turn to for support or in whom they could confide. The significant other was a person who they could trust and who valued them. There was a strong emotional bond between the two. Each seemed to have a vested interest in the other. The significant other influenced their behavior and they in turn sought to please the significant other. Simply stated, the significant other was a person who they perceived as caring about them and whose behavior validated that perception. Mothers and grandmothers were often cast in this role. These strong African-American mothers were perceived as the center of gravity, creating a sense of stability under the most trying of circumstances. They were the architects of strong family networks, creating in their children a sense of mutual obligation, responsibility, and accountability.

Mentoring. Similarly, the storytellers acknowledged the significant role of a mentor in their lives or the perceived need of mentors. They acknowledged the advantages of having a mentor, particularly during the adult years. Unlike the significant other or role model, the mentoring relationship was more explicitly guided by the desire of the mentor to use their expertise to assist the storyteller in reaching a specific goal.

Life transitions. Most of the storytellers could recall a significant event in their lives associated with life stages that served as a stimulus for change. For the female storytellers, change was frequently precipitated by divorce and the need to support their children. For others, the perceived need for change was due to such age-related concerns as having children, graduating from high school, or assessing one's past.

Their stories revealed numerous interrelated variables that contributed to their success in overcoming adversity. They allow the reader to enter their life-world and observe the intricate interplay between these variables and how they make meaning from the world in which they live.

RESISTANCE

Value of negative experiences. Our storytellers' stories suggest that success in overcoming adversity can in part be attributed to how one defines his or her situation. They were generally a very positive lot. Negative experiences were transformed into opportunities for growth. In many instances, negative experiences were perceived as an affront to their sense of dignity and self-esteem. Their response was an all-out assault to conquer or surmount the negative experience to maintain their dignity and self-esteem.

Goal fixation. Each storyteller had a goal in life that was efficacious in keeping them focused. Indubitably, the goal was something they personally valued. Both mental and physical energy was directed toward achieving the goal. There was intrinsic as well as extrinsic motivation to achieve goals. Intrinsic motivation refers to goals they set for themselves based on their personal desires. Extrinsic motivation refers to goals they valued but were pursued, in part, to please a significant other. In most instances, they were clearly intrinsically and extrinsically motivated.

SPIRITUALITY

In general, religion played a significant role in the lives of the storytellers. Religious instruction was part of the early socialization process. In many instances it was quite deliberate with parents themselves instructing the children in the teachings of the Bible. In other instances, religious values were instilled via required church attendance. Religious instruction took a fundamentalist perspective. The Bible was to be lived. Church attendance was perceived as more than a ritualistic exercise in doing the right thing. For some, it was a forum in which talents could be cultivated and skills honed; for others, it was a refuge from the storm. When in need, one could always turn to the church for support. It was fortifying, consistently reaffirming beliefs and values. The church provided the blueprint for living one's life.

Hope. Hope is here defined as the desire for change. It is the belief that one's circumstance, no matter how challenging, can change for the better. The church was the foundation upon which faith, hope, and charity were built. So penetrating was the religious experience that when joy was overshadowed by sadness, and desert streams ran dry, the scripture from the book of Hebrews sprang forth like molten lava to rekindle their spirit: Now faith is the substance of things hoped for, the evidence of things not seen. Our storytellers projected a sense that the power to effect change lies within. There was the realization that mental attitude was as empowering as physical fortitude. Their strong religious conviction seemed to be a significant factor in the evolution of this attitude.

Faith. There was a certain spirituality about the storytellers. Each explicitly articulated a belief in a higher Being with the power (through prayer and faith) to intercede in their lives. It was their belief in God that they credit to their persistence, determination, and resiliency in confronting life's trials and tribulations. Hope was their desire for change and faith their belief that it would happen.

Their stories add to the body of knowledge on triumph over adversity, as they allow a more intrinsic, affective perspective for elucidating the phenomenon. Their stories give renewed meaning to the adage that the past is the foundation upon which the future is built, and that success is not measured by the heights one reaches but by the display of courage in pursuit of the goal.

IMPLICATIONS

The whole is greater than the sum of its parts, for taken collectively, the stories validate, reaffirm, and suggest information that can improve the efficacy of educational programs from preschool to adult education. Within their pages lies valuable information to assist educators in developing programs and teaching methodologies to fulfill their mission. For the African-American community, it offers information to assist in identifying its strengths and using these strengths to empower itself to effect social change and maintain viable communities conducive to success.

Implications for education. The Afrocentric perspective affirms the fact that African-Americans share a common racial experience that sets them apart from other racial groups in this country. In a society where race is imbued with social meaning, the life experiences of African-Americans are colored by their common racial heritage. It is these experiences that, in part, form the foundation of our beliefs and attitudes and that motivate our actions. Therefore, it is important that educators understand the life-world of the African-American. They must understand that meaning can only be understood if we know how people construct reality.

Educators must understand the anger African-Americans feel in educational settings where the contributions to society by their ancestors are ignored or understated. They must break down cultural barriers that perpetuate a belief (conscious or unconscious) in the superiority of one group and cultivate a perception of differences as unique and innovative ways to meet needs and view the world. In doing so, they will create a more meaningful and practical learning environment.

Curriculums must be inclusive, taking into consideration the contributions of people of color and women in all disciplinary areas. A primary consideration in textbook selection should be the degree to which textbooks reflect this reality. Such curriculums will provide fertile ground in which pride in one's culture can take root and an appreciation for the contributions of others to society can be cultivated.

The adult educator can take the first step by developing curriculums that give life to the strengths derived from the African-American experience. The stories in this book offered clear illustrations of these strengths. Through teaching methodologies that give students center stage and the opportunity, in an open forum, to discuss their lives and experiences, adult educators can extract important information to enhance the efficacy of their practice. For example, parenting was a common theme throughout the life histories. Adult education programs can be developed to assist parents in this, the most important role they will play in their children's lives. However, why not depart from textbook formulas to develop a curriculum for such a course and allow the participants through direct participation to develop their own curriculum?

In teacher training institutions more emphasis must be placed on the affective level of instruction. Prospective educators must be sensitized to teaching the whole child or adult. They must seek to know the history and past of their charges. It is only through this knowledge that teachers will understand how their students construct reality and make meaning from the world. This will be the key to understanding behaviors, attitudes, and values. Educators must first accept and respect their charges for who they are and where they are and then, and only then, can the socioeconomic, racial, cultural, or gender barriers be broken down and the path to academic success brought into clear view. They must understand the dynamic that drives an assessment of others. They must understand that in the African-American community much is made of the hidden language of social interaction. It is not so much what is said that is important, but rather the subtle messages received from actions, gestures, voice inflexion, perception of social distance, and words of encouragement or lack of. In this regard, teachers cannot underestimate their impact on students. The power of one negative incident can echo through the corridors of their lives leaving in its wake humiliation, and loss of confidence and self-esteem, unless someone else recognizes the damage and seek to repair it. Educators must seek to expand the boundaries of the curriculum to broaden their students' knowledge and awareness of the world in which they live. They must seek to expose them to the possibilities and equip them with the knowledge, skills, and confidence to reach out and grasp it.

Another theme that pulsated gently beneath the surface of the stories was cultural capital. In the educational setting, African-American students, as it turns out, were not always aware of the resources available to assist them in achieving goals. Many contended that this information blackout was deliberate. What this says to the educator is that not only is there is a need to specifically inform students of available resources but also give instruction in how to access the system to retrieve the resources.

Clearly our storytellers reported more positive experiences with their African-American teachers than their white teachers. A distinguishing characteristic was the level of affective interaction and response. They felt their African-American teachers cared about them personally and perceived them as more than just a student. This was a very interesting dynamic. It went beyond merely being nice. In their own practice and that of preparing adults to work with children, this is a dynamic the adult education practitioner should investigate more thoroughly.

African-American parents must take an active role in monitoring the education of their children, at home and at school. At home, they can ask questions about school, going beyond a mere, "How was school today?" to "What did you learn today?" "Do you have homework?" They can take their children to museums, libraries, on field trips, and if money is a factor, simply turn off the television and talk, play games, after all, necessity is the mother of invention. Some may argue that this is easy for those who need not concern themselves with issues of daily survival. To this I would respond, if we cannot ensure our children a future, then what are we struggling to survive for? We must not allow the fruit to die on the vine. The greatest gift we can give our children is our time and to make them feel valued. This can be accomplished with a word of encouragement, a word of praise, a warm hug, and as our stories revealed a myriad of other subtle or not so subtle ways. Parents can support their children and simultaneously reinforce the importance of education by volunteering at the school, attending activities their children are involved in at school. They can support the school by making it clear to their children why they are there and that disciplinary problems and poor academic performance are unacceptable. They can challenge the school to meet the needs of their children. They can ensure that the curriculum is inclusive and that disciplinary policies are fair and equitable.

The impact of life transitions was noteworthy for the older storytellers. For many, it was the events surrounding life transitions that led them back to the classroom. The adult educator, therefore, has to be cognizant of the extra baggage adults sometimes bring with them. More specifically, adult education programs should offer students support in the form of counseling, tutoring, childcare, facilities to accommodate the physically challenged adult, and support groups to abate the anxiety and lack of confidence characteristic of many returning adults.

Implications for the African-American community. As we traveled through the pages of the lives of our storytellers, we emerge, hopefully, having learned a great deal about how they construct reality and make meaning from their worlds. We experienced them emerge from the valleys to travel the high road. Along the way, they showed us that people as self-learners rely on their own judgment of self, rather than social norms. African- Americans must discover the power within, individually and collectively.

The experiences of our storytellers illustrated the very powerful impact of the black community. Their stories affirm the power of the black community to shape its destiny. The past may hold the key to unlocking a brighter future for our children. The extant black communities would be well advised to revisit the past in a quest for the ties that bind. How can we harness the type of cohesiveness and cooperation in our communities that our storytellers so vividly brought to life in their stories? Clearly, it was a force in creating a sense of stability, hope, and belonging in a society that consistently challenged one's self-esteem and right to exist in the world on equal terms with others.

Much has happened in our society to erode the sense of community in neighborhoods. Disproportionately high unemployment rates among African-American men have contributed to turning our inner cities into vast wastelands of humanity where the landscape is littered with callousness, hopelessness, and despair for all but those who tenaciously wage a daily battle to rise above it. For those who have escaped the ghettos the sense of community remains an elusive ideal. With high rates of mobility, dual income households, and the newness of open housing (which often become re-segregated), neighbors just aren't available to get to know each other. They come together from different places and for the reasons previously mentioned don't get to know each other and form a sense of community. High rates of mobility create an ever changing portrait of the community. The mix is never the same, as in days past when one's roots in the community went back for generations. A sense of this loss can be seen in the modern day inventions of neighborhood watch groups, block clubs, safe houses for latchkey kids, library tutoring programs, big brother, big sister clubs, all seemingly attempts to mold old ideas to fit modern lifestyles. But is it working? Does it have the same impact?

Through our storytellers, we bore witness to the strength of the African-American family and community. In so doing, it sends a clear message to African-Americans that we are sitting on a gold mine. The power of self-determination is within us and all around us. The assistance of government is needed to expidate change; however, it should not be courted at the expense of recognizing the power within. Government can assist by making the ideals of our democratic society a reality, and by creating a level playing field where each player has equal advantage. They can discontinue investing in job training programs for jobs that do not exist or for which the financial benefits barely elevate the worker above the poverty line. Work is one of the ways in which we define ourselves. A giant step toward restoring our inner cities, resurrecting hope, penetrating the darkness of despair, and restoring the self-dignity of the oppressed is to create jobs where people can be gainfully employed.

Perhaps we need to re-examine the old ways and reclaim some of our past. How did we lose the shadow of our past and what has it cost us? To what extent have the traditional African-American values of respect for elders, education, religious practice, and discipline been replaced, attenuated, or modified, and how has this impacted our collective progress and success?

African-American parents must teach their children skills to survive in a society where race still matters. They must be active participants in the lives of their children. They must consciously seek to expose their children to positive role models and hold themselves up as exemplars of the values and attitudes they strive to instill in their children. Parents must teach them about their cultural heritage, connecting them with the well-spring of racial identity and pride. In so doing, they prepare fertile ground for the seeds of achievement and progress to take root and grow.

Home, school, and community must come together in a symbiotic relationship to save our children. As the portrait of the American family has changed over the past decade, there is a pronounced need for such a union. Hardly a day passes without reference in the print or electronic media to African-American children whose lives have been cut short, the direct or indirect victims of violence in the places they call home. Violence that is the spawn of hopelessness and despair. It ricochets through the community, wounding body, mind, and spirit. Home, school, and community must seek to create an environment in which the mental attitude, If I can hope, I can cope, can thrive and bear fruit.

Bibliography

Amato, Paul, and Gary Ochiltree. "Family Resources and the Development of Child Competence." *Journal of Marriage and Family* 48 (1986): 47–56.

Austin, Roy L. "Family Environment, Educational Aspirations and Performance in St. Vincent." *The Review of Black Political Economy* 17 (1989): 101–22.

Bell, Derrick. *Faces at the Bottom of the Well* . New York: Basic Books, 1992.

Billingsley, Andrew. *Black Families in White America*. New Jersey: Prentice-Hall, Inc., 1968.

Blassingame, J. *The Slave Community*. New York: Oxford University Press, 1972.

Blumenthal, Janet. "Mother-Child Interaction and Child Cognitive Development in Low Income Black Children." Paper presented at the biennial meeting of the Society for Research in Child Development (April 1985).

Bogdan, R., and Taylor, S. *Introduction to Qualitative Research Methods*. New York: John Wiley & Sons, 1975.

Brice-Heath, Shirley. "Questioning at Home and at School: A Comparative Study," in *Doing Ethnography Educational Anthropology in Action*. Ed. George Spindler. New York: Holt, Rinehart and Winston, 1982. 96–101.

Bridgeman, B., and H. Burbach. "Effects of Black and White Peer Models on Academic Expectations and Actual Performance on Fifth-Grade Students." *Journal of Experimental Education* 45 (1976): 9–12.

Brown, Cynthia Stokes. *Like It Was: A Complete Guide to Writing Oral History*. New York: Teachers and Writers Collaborative, 1988.

Burgess, M. E. and D. O. Price. *An American Dependency Challenge*. Chicago: American Public Welfare Association, 1963.

Campbell, Bebe. "A Story of Survival." *Essence* (Oct. 1991): 85.

Casey, Kathleen. *I Answer with My Life: Life Histories of Women Teachers Working for Social Change.* New York: Routledge, 1993.

Cartwright, D. S. et al. *Gang Delinquency.* Belmont, CA: Wadsworth, 1975.

Clark, C. "Television and Social Controls: Some Observations on the Portrayal of Ethnic Minorities." *Television Quarterly* 8 (1969): 18–22.

Clark, Reginald. *Family Life and School Achievement: Why Poor Black Children Succeed or Fail.* Chicago: The University of Chicago Press, 1983.

Clark-Stewart, Allison. "Evaluating Parental Effects on Child Development." *Review of Research in Education.* Lee Shulman, ed. Itasca, IL: Peacock, 1978. 47–119.

Cose, Ellis. *The Rage of a Privileged Class.* New York: HarperCollins, 1983.

Datcher-Loury, Linda. "Family Background and School Achievement Among Low Income Blacks." *The Journal of Human Resources* 24 (1989): 528–44.

Davis, Cullom et al. *From Tape to Type: An Oral History Manual and Workbook.* Springfield, Illinois: Oral History Office, Sangamon State University, 1975.

Dimsdale, J. E. "The Coping Behavior of Nazi Concentration Camp Survivors." *Human Adaptation: Coping With Life Crises.* R. H. Moos, ed. Lexington, Massachusetts: D. C. Heath, 1976.

Doob, Christopher B. *Sociology: An Introduction.* 2nd ed. New York: Holt, Rinehart & Winston, Inc., 1988.

Eisner, V. "Effects of Parents in the Home on Delinquency." *Public Health Reports* 81 (1966): 905–10.

Elardo, Richard et al. "The Relation of Infants' Home Environment to Mental Test Performance from Six to Thirty-six Months: A Longitudinal Analysis." *Child Development* 46 (1975): 71–76.

Fedler, F. "The Mass Media and Minority Groups." *Journalism Quarterly* 50 (1973): 109–17.

Freire, Paulo. *Pedagogy of the Oppressed.* New York: Herder and Herder, 1970.

George, L. K. and I. C. Siegler. *Coping With Stress and Coping in Later Life: Older People Speak for Themselves.* North Carolina: Center for the Study of Aging and Human Development and Department of Psychiatry, Duke University Medical Center, 1981.

Glaser, Barney G. and Anselm L. Strauss. *The Discovery of Grounded Theory: Strategies for Qualitative Research.* Chicago: Aldine Publishing Company, 1967.

Greenberg, J. "Children's Reaction to TV Blacks." *Journalism Quarterly* 49 (1972): 5–14.

Greenberg, J., and H. Davidson. "Home Background and School Achievement of Black Urban Ghetto Children." *American Journal of Orthopsychiatry* (1972): 803–10.

Gurin, P., and E. Epps. "Some Characteristics of Students from Poverty Backgrounds Attending Predominantly Negro Colleges in the Deep South." *Social Forces* 45 (1966): 27–39.

Haan, Kurt De, ed. Our Daily Bread. (April 14, 1992) Grand Rapids, Mich.: Radio Bible Class, 1992.

Haley, Alex. *Roots*. New York: Doubleday and Company, Inc., 1976.

Hare, Bruce, and Louis Castenell. "No Place to Run, No Place to Hide: Comparative Status and Future Prospects of Black Boys." *In Beginnings*. Ed Spencer, ed. Brookins and Allen, 1987. 201–14.

Hayes, W. C., and C. H. Mindel. "Extended Kinship Relations in Black and White Families." *Journal of Marriage and Family* 35 (1973): 51–57.

Heatherington, E. Mavis et al. "Achievement and Intellectual Functioning of Children in One-Parent Households."_ In *Achievement and Achievement Motives*. Janet T. Spence, ed. San Francisco: Freeman and Company, 1983.

Heatherington, E. M. "Effects of Father Absence on the Personality Development in Adolescent Daughters." *Developmental Psychology* 7 (1972): 313–26.

Henderson, E. H., and B. H. Long. "Personal-Social Correlates of Academic Success Among Disadvantaged School Beginners." *Journal of School Psychology* 9 (1973): 101–13.

Herzog, Elizabeth and Cecilia E. Sudia. "Children in Fatherless Families."*Child Development Research.* Vol. 4. Bettye M. Caldwell and Henry N. Riccinti, ed. Chicago: University of Chicago Press, 1973.

Hess, Robert et al. "Maternal Variables As Predictors of Children's School Readiness and Later Achievement in Sixth Grade." *Child Development* 55 (1984): 1902–12.

Hoopes, James. *Oral History*. Chapel Hill: University of North Carolina Press, 1979.

Jones-Eddy, Julie. *Homesteading Women: An Oral History of Colorado, 1890-1950*. New York: Twayne Publishers, 1992.

Kandel, D. "Race-Maternal Authority and Adolescent Aspiration." *American Journal of Sociology* 76 (1974): 999–1020.

Keller, S. "The Social World of the Urban Slum Child: Some Early Findings." *American Journal of Orthopsychiatry* 22 (1963): 823–31.

Korner, Stephen. *What Is Philosophy?* London: Allen Lane, 1969.

Kreisberg, L. "Rearing Children for Educational Achievement in Fatherless Families." *Journal of Marriage and Family* 29 (1967): 288–301.

Labov, W., and C. Robbins. "A Note on the Relation of Reading Failure to Peer-Group Status in Urban Ghettos." *Teacher College Record* 70 (1969): 395-405.

Lazarus, R. S. "Little Hassles Can Be Hazardous to Health." *Psychology Today* (July 1981): 58-62.

Leibowitz, Arleen. "Home Investments in Children." *Journal of Political Economy* 82 (1974): 5111-31.

_____. "Parental Inputs and Children's Achievement." *The Journal of Human Resources* 12 (1977): 242-51.

Leifer, A. G. et al. "Children's Television: More than Mere Entertainment." *Harvard Educational Review* 44 (1974): 1213-45.

Lever, D. J. "Sex Differences in the Games Children Play." *Social Problems* 23 (1976): 478-87.

Lincoln, Y. S. and Guba, E. G. *Naturalistic Inquiry.* Newbury Park, California: Sage, 1985.

Lowenthal, M.F. and D. Chiriboga. "Responses to Stress." *Four Stages of Life: A Comparative Study of Men and Women Facing Transition.* M.F. Lowenthal, M. Thurnher, and D. Chiriboga., eds. San Francisco: Jossey-Bass, 1975.

Maehr, M. S. *Sociocultural Origins of Achievement.* Monterey, California: Brooks-Cole, 1974.

McAdoo, H. "The Ecology of Internal and External Support Systems of Black Families." Presented at the Conference on Research Perspectives in the Ecology of Human Development, Cornell University, 1977.

Merchant, Z. "Black Males." *Black Enterprise* 6 (1976): 27-28.

Merriam, Sharan B. *Case Study Research in Education.* San Francisco: Jossey-Bass, 1991.

Mezirow, J. D. "A Critical Theory of Adult Learning and Education." *Adult Education* 32 (1981): 3-23.

Moos, R. H. and V. Tsu. "Human Competence and Coping: An Overview." *Human Adaptation: Coping With Life Crises.* R. H. Moos., ed. Lexington, Massachusetts: Heath, 1976.

Neugarten, B. L. "Adaptation, the Life Cycle." *The Counseling Psychologist* 6.1 (1976): 17.

Noble, P. *Formation of Freirean Facilitators.* Chicago: Latino Institute, 1983.

Nobles, W. W. "The Gift and the Responsibility: Black Father's Role in the Rearing of Our Young." *New Dimensions in Headstart* (Jan. 1974).

Nobles, W. W. "African Roots and American Fruit: The Black Family." *Journal of Social and Behavioral Science* (1974): 20.

Nuttall, R. L. "Some Correlates of High Need Achievement for Urban Northern Negroes." *Journal of Abnormal and Social Psychology* 65 (1964): 593-600.

Ogbu, John. "Origins of Human Competence: A Cultural-Ecological Perspective." *Child Development* 52 (1981): 413–29.

_____. *Minority Education and Caste.* New York: Academic Press, 1974.

Pallone, N. "Key Influences of Occupational Preference Among Black Youth." *Journal of Counseling Psychology* 17 (1970): 498–501.

Pallone, N. et al. "Further Data on Key Influences of Occupational Expectations of Minority Youth." *Journal of Counseling Psychology* 20 (1973): 484–86.

Pearlin, L. I. and C. Schooler. "The Structure of Coping." *Journal of Health and Social Behavior* 19 (1978): 2–21.

Perkins, E. *Home Is a Dirty Street: The Social Oppression of Black Children.* Chicago: Third World Press, 1975.

Peterson, Elizabeth A. *African American Women: A Study of Will and Success.* Jefferson, North Carolina: McFarland & Company, Inc., 1992.

Porter, J. "Race Socialization and Mobility in Educational and Early Occupational Attainment." *American Sociological Review* 39 (1974): 303–16.

Portes, Pedro. "Longitudinal Effects of Early-Age Intervention on Family Behavior." Paper presented at the Annual Meeting of the American Educational Research Association, 1984.

Rosenberg, M. "Which Significant Others?" *American Behavioral Scientist* (1973): 829–59.

Ross, H., and E. Glaser. "Making It Out of the Ghetto." *Professional Psychology* 3 (1973): 347–55.

Scanzoni, J. *The Black Family in Modern Society.* Boston: Allyn and Bacon, 1971.

Schacter, Frances. *Everyday Mother Talk to Toddlers.* New York: Academic Press, 1979.

Schafer, W. E. "Sport and Male Sex Role Socialization." *Sport Sociology Bulletin* 4 (1975): 17–54.

Schlossberg, Nancy K. *Counseling Adults in Transition: Linking Practice With Theory.* New York: Springer Publishing Co., 1984.

Shade, Barbara J. "The Social Success of Black Youth: The Impact of Significant Others. "*Journal of Black Studies* 14.2 (1983): 137–50.

Shade, O. *Significant Other Influence On the Educational Goals of Disadvantaged Afro-American College Freshmen.* Diss. University of Wisconsin, 1978.

Shor, I. *Critical Teaching and Everyday Life.* 2nd Ed. Chicago: University of Chicago Press, 1987.

Silverstein, B., and Krate, R. *Children of the Dark Ghetto.* New York: Praeger, 1975.

Slaughter, Diana T., and Edgar G. Epps. "The Home Environment and Academic Achievement of Black American Children and Youth: An Overview." *Journal of Negro Education* 56.1 (1987): 3–20.

Spiegelberg, H. *The Phenomenological Movement*. The Hague: Martinus Nijhoff, 1965.

Stack, C. *All Our Kin: Strategies for Survival in a Black Community*. New York: Harper and Row, 1974.

Stinnett, S., and J. Wallers. "Parent-Child Relationships of Black and White High School Students: A Comparison." *Journal of Social Psychology* 91 (1973): 349.

Strickland, William. "The Future of Black Men." *Essence* (Nov. 1989): 5.

Strober, Gerald S., and Deborah Strober. *Let Us Begin Anew*. New York: HarperCollins, 1993.

Surlin, S., and Dominick, J. "Television's Function As a Third Parent for Black and White Teenagers." *Journal of Broadcasting* 15 (1971): 70–71.

Thompson, Paul. *The Voice of the Past*. 2nd ed. New York: Oxford University Press, 1988.

Vansina, Jan. *Oral Tradition: A Study in Historical Methodology*. London: Routledge, 1961.

Walker, R. "The Conduct of Educational Case Studies: Ethics, Theory and Procedures." In W. B. Dockerell & D. Hamilton, eds. *Rethinking Educational Research*. London: Hodder & Stoughton, 1980.

Ward, Martha. *Them Children: A Study in Language Learning*. New York: Holt, Rhinehart and Winston, 1971.

Wasserman, H. "A Comparative Study of School Performance Among Boys From Broken and Intact Families." *Journal of Negro Education* 41 (1972): 137–41.

Weiss, R. S. "Transition States and Other Stressful Situations: Their Nature and Programs for Their Management." *Support Systems and Mutual Help: Multidisciplinary Exploration*. G. Caplan and M. Killilea., ed. New York: Grune and Stratton, 1976.

Wickham, DeWayne. "What Drives the Ambitious?" *Black Enterprise* (Jan. 1988): 40–44.

Index

About the Author

GERALDINE COLEMAN and her ten siblings were reared by hardworking and devoted parents who instilled in their children a strong sense of self-worth. She is Associate Principal of Hillcrest High School, as well as a college adult education instructor, in Illinois.